Making Love a Family Affair

Making Love a Family Affair

Family Meditations on Christian Themes

James Weekley

Abingdon Press
Nashville   New York

MAKING LOVE A FAMILY AFFAIR

Copyright © 1974 by Abingdon Press

Library of Congress Cataloging in Publication Data

WEEKLEY, JAMES, 1939-
  Making love a family affair.

  1. Family—Prayer-books and devotions—English.
I. Title.
BV255.W39   242   73-8730

ISBN 0-687-23040-3

New Testament quotations are from Today's English Version
of the New Testament. Copyright © American Bible Society,
1966.

Old Testament quotations are from The Living Bible, © 1971
by Tyndale House Publishers.

The lines of T. S. Eliot on page 13 are from "Four Quartets,"
Collected Poems 1909-1962, and are used by permission of
Harcourt Brace Jovanovich and Faber & Faber, Ltd.

The lines of Edward Arlington Robinson on page 14 are from
"Miniver Cheevy," *Collected Poems,* published by Charles
Scribner's Sons.

MANUFACTURED BY THE PARTHENON PRESS AT
NASHVILLE, TENNESSEE, UNITED STATES OF AMERICA

To our children

Sharyn and Mark
engineers of sandcastles and tinkertoy windmills
enthusiasts of January sledding and July picnics
connoisseurs of cotton candy and Cracker Jacks
guardians of Puff 'n' Stuff kittens and hamster Harry

yet
    nev-
        er
            w
             i
              t
               h
                o
                 u
                  t
                   fill
                   -ing
          our hearts
          with joy,
          our mar-
          riage with ful-
          filment,   and
          our home with
          that   thing
          call-   ed
          love   . . . !

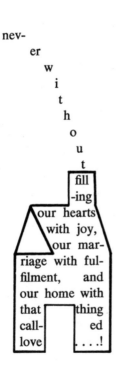

Preface

Isn't it becoming increasingly apparent that the future destiny of our country may hinge greatly upon the extent to which the now-action involvement of our family life is experienced both in the renewal of its inner life and its penetration into the issues of the larger community? However, the dilution of parental authority, the substitution of material securities for family unity, the upsurge in separation-divorce statistics, the heightening generation gap, in fact, accentuate a disturbing pattern in the contemporary American family. As a result of the family's failure to get its own house in order, it has failed to project its energies to the poor, the aged, and company.

Does the American family, then, have a future? The family has survived crises in previous historical ages, but is it capable of coming through with the same score today? There is an ironic thing regarding the profile of the contemporary American family: almost everyone agrees that it's in trouble, but few seem to care enough to do anything significant about it. It's like complaining about pollution but neglecting to become involved in a community task force to clean it up.

Then, too, there are some of us who compromise the situation by latching on to honey-coated-be-kind-to-everybody-a n d-everything-will-work-itself-out recipes of happiness. Let's be honest, we do not need recipes for happy homes today as they promise too much and deliver so little. What the American home desperately needs is a *resource for individual growth* which, in turn, will stabilize family unity. More precisely, it is not families that are failing; it is individual family members who are failing.

Yes, there's a punch line. Let us say that it is here where the Christian gospel truth comes in. It arrives on our secular scene (it always has, you know) with love and justice to pick up the alienated pieces, fuse them with significant meaning, and fill them with a spiritual dynamic necessary for survival (and sanity) in a transitional age.

In the volume to follow we shall attempt to rethink the possibilities of the contemporary family through the dimensions of major Christian themes.

Contents

Making Love a Family Affair

A Word to the Reader

To assemble a group of turned-on kids, a kitchen-PTA-den mother, and a weary dad for a few moments of serious reflection would be nothing short of a minor miracle. What a task it is to shift our schedules into low gear for a few moments of be-still-and-know meditations. Such an experience becomes reminiscent of a frustrated preschooler who was somewhat disappointed with the technique of prayer. Expecting God to answer him in computerized fashion, he commented, "It's no use. Art doesn't listen."

"Art who?" his mother asked?

"Art in heaven," he replied.

But isn't it we who fail to listen patiently to God and one another? I often think that if we're to recover a more sane, purposive family pattern, we're going to have to start with a serene, open-minded patience.

This book attempts to explore some of the key issues family members are thinking about today. Perhaps it would be most profitable to use this book as a resource for family meditations during one evening in the middle of the week. The mother or father may wish to take turns reading the meditations. Also, spontaneous questions may be raised at the conclusion in order to stimulate discussion.

Dag Hammarskjöld reminds us as families: "In our era the road to holiness necessarily passes through the world of action." Meditative action, as it were, is one giant step forward necessary for mankind's renewal and redemption. The world demands stronger families with Christ-minded postures. For we as Christians have his truth before us, and that truth can set us free to be authentically human.

The Possible Dream

The New Year

When anyone is joined to Christ he is a new being:
the old is gone, the new has come.

II Cor. 5:17

The eclipse from the gaiety of Christmas to the
sober reflection on the New Year leaves one with
mixed feelings of anxiety and frustration. This ex-
perience-in-transition is reflected in T. S. Eliot's
verse.

> What we call the beginning is often the end
> And to make an end is to make a beginning.
> The end is where we start from.

Well, standing somewhat confused like a double-
faced Janus, we as Christian families ponder the
obvious question, "Where do we go from here—
that is, if we care to go at all?" I suppose the past
retains a peculiar charm about itself which we all
relish for any number of reasons. For one thing this
once-removed element of time flashes back memo-
rable events which become permanent fixtures in

our minds such as family outings and achievements in school and on the job. Then, too, the past can become an instant escape machine from reality to fantasy. Do you remember Edwin Arlington Robinson's interesting little character, Miniver Cheevy?

> Miniver Cheevy, born too late,
>   Scratched his head and kept on thinking;
> Miniver coughed, and called it fate,
>   And kept on drinking.

Also, the contemplation of the past may give us an excuse to lament over tarnished opportunities and shallow immaturities. As such the past becomes therapeutic and redemptive only if we achieve a more responsible mature growth.

With reference to this growth possibility, John's Gospel records a unique happening between Jesus and Nicodemus: "How can a grown man be born again?" Nicodemus asked. "He certainly cannot enter his mother's womb and be born a second time!" "I tell you the truth," replied Jesus, "that no one can enter the Kingdom of God unless he is born of water and the Spirit" (3:4-5). According to Jesus, then, rebirth, a growth process from past to present, is made possible only by the reception of God's Spirit into our total life pattern. God also requires us to renounce past errors and start anew. Thereupon, we become men and women of the now, who grow through the dimensions of faith, hope, and love.

14

The security and happiness of the contemporary family has a great stake in the spiritual renewal-growth process of its individual members. The whole is as great as its parts. "Instead, by speaking the truth in a spirit of love, we must grow up in every way to Christ, who is the head. Under his control all the different parts of the body fit together, and the whole body is held together by every joint with which it is provided. So when each separate part works as it should, the whole body grows and builds itself up through love" (Eph. 4:15-16).

Prayer: Lord, spare us of entering the New Year unprepared. Do give us, however, the insight to remake our homes into shelters of security against the confusing storms of change. Amen.

becomes a powerful and inspiring king. A tent-maker becomes a renowned author. A stubborn fisherman becomes a church architect.

Even before Abraham Lincoln became president, he had been defeated in business twice, lost a seat in the state legislature once, the House of Representatives once, and the U.S. Senate twice. On top of this, he suffered a nervous breakdown. God is a champion of lost causes, often led by slumbering has-beens who courageously build on the ashes of their failures. He has a unique way of preserving men and women for a particular moment of greatness in history. Have we allowed him to awaken our faith to the exciting venture of spiritual renewal in our church?

And second, spiritual church renewal will require an unconditional acceptance of the Holy Spirit. As Eutychus' life was directly dependent upon the renewing power of God's Spirit, so our life as Christians requires a consistent injection of God's presence. Through the medium of prayer and Bible study, for example, we become God-inflated men and women cleansed by his grace and renewed through his love. Carl F. H. Henry outlines our ministry of love as Christian families in a renewing church: "Our calling as Christians is to take the whole Gospel to the whole world, with an evangelism rooted in the power of Pentecost and a social passion guided by the vision of the prophets."

Prayer: Lord, the Creator and Sustainer of all biological life, renew us with an exciting Spirit. Without access to your Spirit, how could we hope to become your authentic church? Amen.

But I Gave at the Office

Stewardship of Possessions

Bring all the tithes into the storehouse so that there
will be food enough in my Temple; if you do, I will
open up the windows of heaven for you and pour
out a blessing so great you won't have room enough
to take it in!   Mal. 3:10

It is estimated that Americans spend more than
two hundred dollars on military hardware and per-
sonnel for every dollar we invest in maintaining a
national morality. And many of us are so naïve as
to ask, "Why has the crime rate risen so sharply?
Why are racial wounds and generation gaps forged
into the conscience of our nation? Why have we,
the wealthiest and most productive nation on earth,
inherited a national debt of approximately 400 bil-
lion dollars?"

To a great extent our national crisis can be
traced to the failure of the church to come through
at points with authentic spiritual goods for modern
man during the past few decades. As such, the crisis

cuts beneath the church's shaky statistics and the decline of a more dedicated ministry to a much deeper source: a distorted conception of Christian stewardship. Jesus pinpoints our problem when he said, "Watch out, and guard yourselves from all kinds of greed; for a man's true life is not made up of the things he owns, no matter how rich he may be" (Luke 12:15). By cheating God in our stewardship of possessions, we have shortchanged our own faith and its potential impact upon our society. If possible, how may we reclaim this prodigal sense of Christian stewardship?

One, we must reevaluate our *obligations to God*. To be honest, do we as Americans really appreciate what God has done for us as a nation? Did not such an attitude compel Moses to lay it on the line to the stubborn Hebrews?

When the Lord your God has brought you into the land he promised your ancestors, Abraham, Isaac, and Jacob, and when he has given you great cities . . . you didn't build, wells you didn't dig, and vineyards and olive trees you didn't plant—and when you have eaten until you can hold no more, then beware lest you forget the Lord who brought you out of the land of Egypt, the land of slavery (Deut. 6:10-12).

As strange as it may seem, God doesn't need our money. What he is really after is a dedicated heart.

Two, we must rethink our *relationship with our church*. We are reminded in I Peter: "Each one, as a good manager of God's different gifts, must

21

use for the good of others the special gift he has received from God" (4:10).

In a day when each of us is caught in the spiral of inflation, many church families are asking, "How much should we give to the support of the church? Obviously, this is a matter of conscience. Yet the Christian conscience becomes satisfied only when one subscribes to systematic and abundant giving, remembering that tithing was ordained by God (Lev. 27:30) and commanded by Jesus himself (Matt. 23:23). Only then do the rewards of a high-geared stewardship open up: happiness, peace of mind, God-given health, plus a more disciplined style of spiritual living.

And three, we must reconsider the *power of our faith*. Jesus said, "For your heart will always be where your riches are" (Luke 12:34). What we give in fact reflects our faith productivity. Without the challenge of stewardship in our total Christian experience, how else could our faith grow and mature?

Prayer: Help us to see, Father, that religion really works. Through our examples, may our children and youth discover that spiritual investments pay the greatest dividends. Isn't tithing a good beginning? Amen.

Puff 'n' Stuff

Materialism

For the bread that God gives is he who comes down
from heaven and gives life to the whole world.

John 6:33

Once upon a biblical time, there lived a successful man who earned his living from the land. He
became so wealthy that he found it necessary to
rebuild his food storage plants. Having become intrigued with this bright idea he thought to himself, "Man, you have it made! Look at what you've
accomplished: a cozy nest egg wrapped up neatly
in a life of ease and comfort. Who wouldn't want to
be in your shoes?"

Immediately, however, his flight of fantasy was
grounded by a voice from a higher dimension, "Listen, you're dreaming up a fool's paradise. In fact
you'll never live to see it, because tonight you're going to die—and you can't take it with you, either!"
Then the great teacher Jesus concluded, "This is
how it is with those who pile up riches for them-

selves but are not rich in God's sight" (Luke 12:21).

The old Protestant ethic operated on an assumption opposite this spiritual truth of Jesus, namely, hard work is virtue and subsequent financial success is God's reward. And in great measure the American Dream was erected on this premise, and it figured in the taming of the frontier. Now we're in the seventies and another myth has been pricked. At least to Christians who bank on the teachings of Jesus in transitional times, a new Christian ethic (or shall we say a reemphasis of the old) has become more evident. Thanks to our youth, who are beginning to see practical merit in the timeless truths of the Christian religion, the accumulation of sophisticated material trinkets is no longer the highest good in life. A youth from Whittier College recently commented, "I came from a poor family, but I've always been able to get the things I want through hard work. As I go into life I want something challenging. Making money was a challenge for my parents, but, for better or worse, it's not that way any more."

Let us consider this question as a family: Are we too cushioned with security? Do we really need all the material items in our possession? As such perhaps we've lost a great portion of our spiritual vision as Christians. None of us would doubt the necessity of material goods in our lives. For one thing, they are capable of becoming a means to the end of happiness—both for ourselves and for unfortunate others. But the catch is that we reach a point where we are so hung-up on what we have accumulated, we switch off God and the broken needs of our neighbor, then we become like T. S. Eliot's hollow man, stuffed with lifeless material straw.

The youth of the current generation want no part of a life which grows sluggish on material apathy and greed. Irwin Edman says. "Show me men and women in whom luxury and worldliness are present, and you will show me an age in which authentic life [diminishes], you will show me men and women in whom spirit dies and is utterly destroyed." Jesus cautions us as Christian families: "Do not save riches here on earth, where moths and rust destroy, and robbers break in and steal. Instead, save riches in heaven, where moth and rust cannot destroy, and robbers cannot break in and steal. For your heart will always be where your riches are" (Matt. 6:19-21).

Prayer: The "things" game gains little yardage, Lord. The critical problems and issues of life are tackled successfully only through dedicated hard work. Keep us aware of this, Lord. Amen.

Bringing Us Together

Race Relations

Do for others what you want them to do for you.
Matt. 7:12

For Christians, Brotherhood Week can become quite frustrating. For one thing this observance can symbolize the shallowness of white America's conception of the Negro, the Mexican American, the Indian, the Puerto Rican. Often we want someone to bug our consciences just enough to make us feel a little guilty for our sins of racial injustice. But when we are challenged to prove ourselves worthy by involving our energies in community programs for the deserving poor, that's when most of us prefer to pass by on the other side. It becomes what Donald McEvoy suggests: "Taking aspirin to treat cancer of the soul."

Also, brotherhood week can become disillusioning in that it indicates a twisted sense of values—a colossal whitewash job in Christian morality. For instance, in a typical race relations sermon or study, one is tempted to conclude a one-sided view of Christian truth by blasting black militants who pursue rip-the-establishment-to-pieces philosophy without acknowledging the perpetuation of lukewarm, do-nothing attitude on the part of white Americans.

So where does this leave us? It leaves us with a great deal of soul-searching. And it must begin in our families with an honest examination of the feelings many of us retain toward our Negro (white) brother and sister. Only then will individual healing and national peace come more quickly. It is our Christian responsibility to create beginnings in racial understanding—even though change is not always easy to accept. And racial understanding and cooperation must begin in the home itself. It must begin foremost with parents and wholesome attitudes of goodwill and kindness and must continue with concrete action.

For the white American this will involve a once-and-for-all burial of such misconceptions about his black/brown/red/yellow brothers as: They are second-rate human beings who are unappreciative of the opportunities afforded them the past decade. To the contrary, a vast majority of minority Americans believe in America, cherish its principles of democracy and are reasonably patient in spite of discrimination.

The minority American, on the other hand, must meet his white brothers and sisters halfway by discarding (not repressing) any feelings of bitterness and hatred toward white neighbors, by extending the hand of forgiveness to those who have afflicted him unjustly, and by maintaining an open-minded understanding in efforts with all Americans to make liberty and justice for all a reality. A Negro college student recently confessed: "How can I hate white people when there are white people like Annette and George whom I love . . . who have taken the time to know me, who have helped me live, and who have accepted people for what they are, because of the love of Christ has given them?" Baron von Hügel summed it up: "Christ has taught us to care—caring is the great thing; caring matters most."

Prayer: Didn't Martin Luther King, Jr. once say: "Either we live together like brothers, or we will perish like fools"? As brothers, Father, give us the strength to arise at the command of your love rather than falling prey to group hatreds. Amen.

Listen, Lord, It's Me!

Prayer

The prayer of a righteous man has a powerful effect.   James 5:16

Is it either reasonable or practical to pray in an age such as ours? Why pray for rain when we can employ the chemical techniques of aerial rainmaking? Yet if some of us practice prayer at all, it only becomes a panic button, a plea to pull us through an emergency situation. And even then—if God is the cosmic super Power Christianity submits him to be—is it really necessary to address him since he knows our every wish anyway? Can we really expect God to toy with economic conditions, political systems, and natural laws for our own interests? In a sense not, for such divine acts would be escape hatches from our responsibilities as moral creatures. God isn't going to accomplish anything spectacular for us that we aren't capable of doing for ourselves.

However, there are situations when our efforts become so exhausting that, unless we secure the resources of divine spiritual assistance, our aspirations become futile. Here is where, in the midst of desperation and agony, unselfish prayer (in conjunction, of course, with God's purpose for our lives) miraculously alters and transforms human dimensions. We cannot explain in biological terms, for example, the remarkable healing of a patient with an incurable cancer physicians had earlier diagnosed as terminal. We only know that a supreme Power injects healing presence into the diseased cells and restores their natural life-sustaining processes.

Prayer, then, is functional. It delivers. The dramatic personalities of biblical history were at best men of prayer. Prayer gave Abraham the vision of a new covenant; Moses the courage to secure "freedom now"; Jesus the power to establish a new religion of the foundations of eternal love and human faith. Through their disciplined prayer experiences, God became a living reality in their daily life pulse.

What about us as a family? Is prayer just a handy tool to have around, or is it, like breathing, a continuous experience? Does it express our deepest desires, or does it ring with an artificial stained-glass image?

If prayer is to work effectively in our home, we must approach it with utmost seriousness. In faith we must honestly believe that the act of prayer is "for real." As Christ acknowledged that prayer was a basic ingredient in Christian growth, we should likewise maintain confidence in what he can accomplish through us in our conversations with him. How does prayer influence individual Christian growth?

For one thing, prayer *checks our immaturities.* It is unfortunate that we as parents have often failed to outgrow preadolescent mannerisms such as hot tempers. It is unfortunate because our children and youth may duplicate these habits. Prayer, like a mirror, reflects back upon us our failings. By honestly spilling our hearts upon God's presence, we confess: "Lord, I failed again. Forgive me and I will try to improve the next time."

Also, prayer *sharpens our spiritual vision.* Confession compels us to quit feeling sorry for ourselves and get with the business of living and serving others. It is at this point that we appreciate more fully the vastness of God's forgiving love and our functional role in his divine enterprise. From the depths of our souls the light of his presence sets our sights on life's intrinsic values, and we affirm with Malcolm Boyd: "This is a good day for me. Yesterday I was down, but today I'm up again. . . . The sun has really come out for me."

Prayer: Our heavenly Father, we acknowledge our lack of discipline and compassion in our prayers. Enable us to see that shortcuts in prayer usually lead to an undercutting of our faith. Amen.

Spring Training

Lent

For sin pays its wage—death; but God's free gift is eternal life in union with Christ Jesus our Lord.

Rom. 6:23

Once in a gay English garden a contest took place. It was the queen's croquet game, and that made it extraordinary. Although the queen had plenty of competition, she always managed to win. In the heat of the contest one of her competitors, Alice, commented to the Cheshire cat; "She's so extremely likely to win that it's hardly worthwhile finishing the game."

Unlike the queen's summer past time, Lent is not a legalistic marathon to be played, but an experience to be endured. The observance of Lent calls our attention to the fact that, in order to overcome the power of evil at all times, we should make a conscious effort to get the upper hand during a forty-day period. Lent puts it simply: "Show me how tough your faith really is." If our faith fails to live up to its potential during the Lenten period, then how can we expect it to function successfully at other times? This is frightening, isn't it? But did not Jesus make it clear when he suggested that the entire business of discipleship is a twelve-month affair?

To the Hebrew man, sin was conceived as missing the mark of God's perfected holiness. In the New Testament Jesus did not attempt to explain the nature of sin. He simply acknowledged its reality and provided guidelines as to how it might be handled.

Whether we wish to admit it or not, modern man is essentially arrogant regarding the issue of sin: "Look, I've come a long way from Genesis 2. Why worry about sin and forgiveness? Science and technology is the name of the game now. So who needs God?"

But to the Christian sin is not a casual issue to be yawned at; it is a reality to be coped with. Otherwise, we open ourselves to its deadly and corruptive forces.

How, then, may we deal with the problem of sin in our lives—particularly during this Lenten period? What particular guidelines would Jesus suggest at this point?

To begin with Jesus calls for self-examination. "If anyone wants to come with me, he must forget himself, take up his cross every day, and follow me" (Luke 9:23). This experience of self-analysis can become quite humbling. It's not always easy to admit that you're wrong.

One of the important functions of the family is the sharing of one's problems in honesty and love. If we are courageous enough to expose our weaknesses to the warmth and strength of family unity, productive growth and renewal take place.

Moreover, Jesus challenges us to hook up on his *power frequency.* "Dear friends! Let us love one another, for love comes from God. Whoever loves is a child of God and knows God" (I John 4:7). The thing to note about this incredible power is you cannot possibly understand it until you experience it. Most of the world knows love by definition, but few of us know it as a natural experience. In what ways is love experienced in our home?

Prayer: "We shall overcome!" Isn't this the theme of Lent, Lord? Without a struggle against temptations from within and secularism from without, how can our faith expect to come out on top? Strengthen us with love. Amen.

Putting Faith Back into Style

Faith

He who is put right with God through faith shall live.   Rom. 1:17

Raymond Schuessler tells of a diabetic who, after hearing of a secret new remedy called the magic spike, went and paid $306 for it. The so-called remedy was nothing more than a pencil-sized tube of barium chloride which was worth less than a penny. The following instructions were attached, "Hang this around your neck, and its rays will cure any disease you have." Unfortunately, this person died in diabetic coma because he placed his trust in the wrong source.

Are most of us so naïve that we latch onto every dream which comes along with no questions asked? Can we, as a popular song suggests, be living in a world where anything that goes wrong can be swept away, and things be kept sweet with cologne? Thank God we live in a more realistic world. To be sure, the Christian is familiar with this world

God has created: a planet with countless possibilities for fulfillment, but not without endurance and hardship. What, then, is the Christian's secret of success in this venture? Is it faith? We had better believe it!

In Edward Albee's play, *Tiny Alice,* Brother Julian, who had spent six years in an asylum, affirms: "My faith is my sanity." Really, the Christian religion is the only certainty we possess in a papier-mâché society of false promises. It stands alone in its field with these try-me-and-see credentials: "I am the way, I am the truth, I am the life" (John 14:6). It even dares to make the claim: "To have faith is to be sure of the things we hope for, to be certain of the things we cannot see" (Heb. 11:1).

Most important, faith is capable of creating disciplined lives within the family unit itself. The crucial problems of the church today inevitably stem from an insufficient amount of spiritual discipline among its constituents. And until we recognize that individual need is of higher priority than elaborate structures and formats, the church will continue to diminish in influence in our society. There are no shortcuts to a life of disciplined prayer, Bible study, and meditative reflection. It simply requires time and effort.

Faith also directs us to where the action is. The Christian, who functions from a disciplined faith, experiences a life-style of exciting meaning. Dietrich Bonhoeffer wrote from a Nazi prison: "Make up your mind and come out into the tempest of living. God's command is enough and your faith in him to sustain you. Then at last freedom will welcome your spirit amid great rejoicing."

Nicholas Murray Butler reminds us that the world consists of people: a small group who makes things happen, a larger group who watches things happen, and a great multitude who never know what happens. The ultimate test of faith is disclosed only in the minority of Christians who make faith happen through action-now involvement.

Prayer: Dear God: Forgive us for checkmating our faith with the pawns of fear and doubt. Stir us until our faith becomes more responsive to your moves within us and our moves toward others. Amen.

The Media of the Cross

Words from the Cross

Be glad that you are sharing Christ's sufferings.
I Pet. 4:13

Basic human needs and drives never change. They have been infused into our anatomy since creation. Although our needs may vary in degree according to the dictates of the times, essentially they are unchangeable. Even amid the horror of Jesus' agony and pain, he disclosed, through the media of his Father's love, his basic needs both as a human being and as the Son of God. On the Cross, then, Jesus revealed the seven basic needs of mankind.

1. Forgiveness

Forgive them, Father! They don't know what they are doing.

Luke 23:34

One of the unique features Jesus introduced in his ministry was the dual function of forgiveness: men and women become worthy of God's forgiveness only when they are willing to forgive others (see Eph. 4:32). The capacity to forgive is a vital ingredient necessary for marital and family success. When family members are willing to dismiss one another's failings, trust emerges.

2. Eternity

I tell you this: today you will be in Paradise with me.

Luke 23:43

Biblical man was intrigued with the concept of the afterlife. But then Jesus came along and turned things upside down. To Jesus, heaven was where God's presence was experienced in joy. In order to survive these difficult times, families must secure a portion of heaven, God's presence, in their homes.

3. Motherhood

Woman, here is your son. . . . Here is your mother.

John 19:26, 27

During his final moments of rejection, Jesus sensed, perhaps more than anything else, the faithful love of Mary his mother. One of the basic needs of America today is more dedicated and caring mothers who place husband and children before materialism.

39

4. Alienation

My God, my God, why did you abandon me?
Matt. 27:46

With these words Jesus expressed the deep agony that God had forgotten him. These words apply to us as families. We need each other in difficulty. A family that has the courage to work through problems together, stays together.

5. Thirst

I am thirsty.

John 19:28

Jesus was constantly offering a cup of water to those parched by thirst. Now on the Cross some of them rewarded him with a taste of vinegar. The living Christ reminds us that in him we will never thirst for warm friendship and spiritual fellowship.

6. Death

It is finished!

John 19:30

Death is not curtains. Within the span of three days Jesus gave death windows. It is tragic that millions of American families are unprepared when death comes to their homes. We must teach our children that death is not to be feared. It is a celebration of life.

7. Hope

Father! In your hands I place my spirit!
Luke 23:46

Jesus ministry was hope-oriented. Christian families are composites of people with hope. Our hope should be fulfilled in service to others.

Prayer: Enable us to understand, Father, that the Cross is more than a token symbol of your Son's suffering and death. May we observe that his cross monitors a challenge to discipleship. Amen.

The Celebration on Main Street

Palm Sunday

"Praise to David's Son! God bless him who comes in the name of the Lord! Praise be to God!"

Matt. 21:9

As a playful creature man is fond of festivals. He proposes every excuse possible to hold one, even if it's nothing more than to celebrate celebrating. Of course, his sophisticated play ranges from the ridiculously sensuous to the highly religious.

Although Jesus was no bluenose, he certainly enjoyed a good time—an experience which promoted warm fellowship and spiritual fulfillment. His first miracle took place at a wedding party. In his parables he would reflect upon a great feast and a lost youth returning to a rejoicing father.

Then, at the conclusion of his ministry, his great moment of celebration came. The occasion was the Passover feast, the commemoration of God's deliverance of the ancient Hebrews from the dictatorship of Pharaoh. On this event expectations were riding high. Would God pull it off again? they wondered. "Would he send another Moses to liberate them from the power of Rome and re-establish another Davidic kingdom? Would Zechariah's prophecy become fact? "Tell the city of Zion: Now your king is coming to you, He is gentle and rides on a donkey" (Matt. 21:5).

"Who would the Messiah be?" they asked. "But look, it's that young teacher from Nazareth. He's riding on a donkey, too!" The streets of Jerusalem lit up with emotional frenzy and joy. The crowd spread their cloth banners before him and waved their palm peace symbols as he passed.

As Americans living twenty centuries removed from that first palm parade, we, too, ponder the question, "Who is this Jesus?" The real question however, is not who, but where. Most of us know who Jesus is. But we do not always know (or more honestly we are afraid to know) *where* he addresses us amid the varied situations of our daily life experiences. Like Judas some of us evade the question for other priorities such as an obsession with materialism. Like Pilate we toy with the question momentarily, but just as quickly give in to the frantic demands of conventionalism. Like Peter we are fearful of the risks of being caught cold with the hero long after the glamor of the parade has been forgotten.

Isn't this one of the difficulties we Christians have in a secular society? Everybody loves a winner as

43

long as he doesn't get into foul trouble. We fail to see beyond the parade of celebration to the Crucifixion with its risks of suffering, committed living, and sacrificial giving. The ride-on-Jesus-I-like-it-where-I-am spectator role is less demanding than the participant role of faith and love. Yes, the Christian life must embody parades of rejoicing (worship), yet never without agonizing Golgothas and subsequent Easter hope.

Prayer: We celebrate the humanity and the divinity of your Son, Father. We thank you for his exciting presence among us. Christ is love! Christ is here! Christ is now! Amen.

Has Suffering Had It?

Holy Week

In everything we do we show that we are God's servants, by enduring troubles, hardships, and difficulties with great patience.

II Cor. 6:4

With the recent discovery of wonder drugs and the assurance of reliable hospitals in our communities, it would appear as if medical science has virtually conquered suffering. Yet it isn't quite that simple. Although physical suffering has been greatly reduced in recent years, with the increased pressures and demands of our society human agony seems to be greater than ever. That is to say, other forms of suffering have emerged with a greater degree of intensity and complexity.

There is the emotional dimension of suffering. We may perceive this anguish in parents who live with the uncertainty of a son at war; a high school student who doesn't know what to do with his or her life; children in orphanages who see other children with parents and wonder why they don't have any.

There is also a spiritual dimension of suffering. For example, this level of suffering exists in the lives of alcoholics or youth on other drugs who turn to the church for a greater love and acceptance, but are discouraged by its sometimes pious remedies: "Have faith and everything will take care of itself." Or in a housewife living in a lonely prison of screaming children, desperately wanting someone to talk to.

Certainly, all of us are familiar with these forms of suffering in greater or lesser measure. And during this Holy Week when we reflect upon Christ's suffering on our behalf, we ask, "How may we adequately handle suffering?"

First, we should face suffering by *ourselves*. This is the most difficult stage in the suffering process. When it hits us unexpectedly we are caught by surprise. Then we begin to realize that we must learn to live with it the best way possible. We must have the faith to cope positively with suffering whenever the situation arises. Dietrich Bonhoeffer defines the nature of our suffering: Suffering has to be endured in order that it may pass away."

Second, we should face suffering with *God*. How many of us have endured suffering to the point where we felt we couldn't take it any longer? Did we turn to God for assistance by saying: "Lord, it's in your hands now. I have faith in your healing power?" Let us recall the words of his Son at this point: "Come to me, all of you who are tired from carrying your heavy loads, and I will give you rest." (Matt. 11:28). It is only our faith and God's presence that can redirect our suffering into the channels of peace and understanding. More importantly, perhaps, suffering is in effect a gauge which determines the active level of our maturity in the love of Christ.

Prayer: Lord, you suffered without complaint. We complain if we suffer even a little. How can we identify with you without occasional anguish? Help us to accept pain and suffering with grace. Amen.

The Hope Dimension

Easter

Just as Christ was raised from death by the glorious power of the Father, so also we might live a new life.

Rom. 6:4

"Why do people die, Daddy? What happens to them after they are put into the ground?" These were two loaded questions my five-year-old son fired at me after observing a burial in our church cemetery. To a minister who is exposed to terminal illinesses and death almost daily, these were run-of-the-mill questions, but to Mark they were quite real and very puzzling.

The shock of death and the subsequent grief experience are difficult enough for adults to cope with. Imagine how much more difficult it becomes for children to understand. Death, then, is a real threat to children.

To begin with, death threatens the emotional security of children because in itself death is counter-life. It throws things into a horrifying skid. At least during the past few decades our children have been bombarded with the onesided life principle from the media: the Mary-Poppins-gingerbread-cola-Saturday-morning-cartoon ethic that suggests that one should get all he can out of life (good so far), but which totally ignores pain, alienation, and, of course, death. Secret Squirrel and Bad Lands Sam always get shot at, but they never get killed (chalk another one up for Batman and Robin).

Death also threatens children because it plays havoc on their sensitive feelings and emotions. They simply cannot handle the shock experience by themselves. Their reactions range anywhere from anger and nightmares to the sensation that grief experiences are bad—hence, such experiences become repressed into guilt and cause further (often permanent) emotional pain. He or she may fear that a grandparent or another loved one may soon die, too.

In order that our children may accept death as a natural segment of life and successfully feel their way through the difficult grief experience, we as parents must help them. Casual answers to their perplexing questions and pious clichés—"Have faith, son, and God will take care of it all"—only reassure them that one must have little responsibility in the grief experience. Jesus did not evade this difficult experience. As a human being with an

49

intense capacity for compassion, he wept for Lazarus. In death experiences, we as parents must express our grief feelings mutually, otherwise our children may have difficulty in releasing and sharing their guilt with us. If, on the other hand, our children know that in crises situations they can turn to us for love and trust, their disturbing questions and tattered feelings will be reinforced with meaning and understanding.

More positively, our task as parents will be to help our children see that death isn't artificial, but natural and quite real; that death is not to be feared, but accepted as a significant dimension of living where maturity can be deepened; that death is not to be isolated as unpleasant, but that grief is to be expressed in an atmosphere of acceptance; that people do not die primarily as a result of old age, but die because they cease to retain the will to live and to keep their minds and bodies active and alive after age sixty-five.

So as supportive figures we must become instruments of hope and strength; understanding and sharing, but always acting, too. For we become involved with death by replacing our loss with stronger family ties and by doing more things together.

Isn't this really what Easter is all about: the *celebration* of authentic spiritual life *together* in the midst of even death? "But you know him, for he remains with you and lives in you" (John 14:17).

Prayer: Why do we reserve the celebration of Christ's resurrection for Easter Sunday only, Father? Is his resurrection too powerful for us to handle the remaining 364 days? Awaken us, Father, to his rebirth! Amen.

Handle with Care

Emotions

He placed his hands on her and at once she
straightened herself up and praised God.

Luke 13:13

One of the threats to my life occurred in a sensitivity training group among fellow seminary stu-
dents and our wives. Within that "gut" context each
of us was forced to let individual feelings hang out.
Each of us felt threatened because each was fearful
of discovering the person he or she really was. In
an effort to conceal our true identities, we threw up
all sorts of defensive mechanisms like ill-timed body
movements and facial mannerisms. Yet, after the
first few sessions, we did become more sensitive
both to our own feelings and the feelings of one
another. Within just a few weeks we observed rebirth and renewal of our inner selves.

Of course, it would be difficult for many of us as
family members to function formally together on a
level of such intense feeling because of the threat

52

to our authority as parents, the immature feelings of our children, and even such trivial considerations as conflicting schedules. However, this does not mean that we cannot try to rediscover and renew our feelings more intimately as a family organism.

Perhaps we could begin by becoming more perceptive listeners. Have you ever wondered, amid the crossfire of blasting stereos and teen chatter, why our once sane existence has come to this, why the human mind tolerates such audio bombardments eight to ten hours a day? Could it be that our problem lies in the fact that we have become so conditioned to hearing sounds, that we have failed to listen to human feelings? The extended hours of TV viewing, for example, become our crutch so that we may evade confrontations of need and suffering with other family members.

Predictably, the most frequent criticism parents have of one another today is their failure to communicate or to listen fully. Basically, we fail to listen because of our preoccupation with self-interests and nagging worries. On the other hand, one of the reasons Jesus was so unique must have been his perceptive ability to listen. He penetrated the other person's outer mask and zeroed in on the inner being. By reaching out he touched. By touching he communicated warmth. By caring he helped others listen. Then miracles happened.

Families may also mature on the feeling level by acquiring a more honest openness in their communications with one another. Our feelings are not islands unto themselves; we must continually seek out other's feelings for trust and understanding. Our feelings often become brittle because we hang them up for too long a period of time. This was the threatening pain we experienced in our sensitivity group; and only by honestly sharing our inner selves did our feelings become more stabilized with acceptance. As families we must take the time to sit down frequently and rap. There is no substitute for this form of discipline.

Moreover, families may renew their feelings on an intimate level by rediscovering the therapy of joy. We must once again develop a sense of humor and a greater enthusiasm for living. Employing the language of touch (warmth) in our relationships, group activities, games (acceptance), and devotional experiences together are positive steps in this direction.

Prayer: What has happened to us, Lord? We feel but do not touch; hear but fail to listen; talk but do not speak. Come to us, Lord, and touch us—heal us—that we may become authentically human again. Amen.

Action Now!

A Family Task Force

This is how it is with faith: if it is alone and has no actions with it, then it is dead.

James 2:17

Parents usually underestimate the influence they have upon their children. I recall an incident in our home during the early fifties when my father, my brother, and myself took baskets of food to an impoverished family. It impressed me as a young boy because, frankly, I didn't think that the church usually did things like that. For the first time in my life, I saw raw human need. And it took a family project (we didn't call it a task force in those days) to make this clear to me.

Norman Cousins reminds us that at this point "the biggest lesson of all to be learned about contemporary civilization is that nothing anyone is doing today makes any sense unless it is connected to the making of a genuine peace." Our family can contribute significantly to this peacemaking task

55

by becoming more involved with the problems about us—perhaps just down the street. For authentic togetherness in any home is best realized through activities that are extra-family centered.

Let us now address ourselves to the question of how we can actually accomplish this as a family unit. Here is where family service projects come into the picture. In fact this thrust is the voluntary act of responding to the critical needs of persons and families in our immediate community. We will now consider the following steps as possibilities:

(a) *Motivation:* Do we have a sincere desire to share our love with another family?

(b) *Research:* This is the effort of studying our community (usually within a five-mile radius) for possible needs. Local churches and county social service departments can be of assistance in this effort.

(c) *Legitimacy:* Who qualifies as a recipient of our concern and assistance? A widow supporting four children represents an unqualified need, whereas the need of a man too indolent to work is questionable under many circumstances.

(d) *Involvement:* Getting the job done with ourselves in the center of the action. Christian involvement entails more than a five-minute visit. Disadvantaged people do have pride and human feelings. They need our understanding, not pity.

(e) *The Follow-Up:* By continually following up our visits to these people, we will soon prove that our concern is authentic. And this is where our love power is gauged. The job of reconciliation certainly cannot be completed overnight. Perhaps it will involve a weekly visit over a two-year period.

To be honest, most families today expect a professional do-gooder to manipulate the gears on the machinery of reconciliation. Isn't this precisely the predicament of many churches, as well? We do not want to soil our nicely manicured hands with the grime of involvement in cooling the racial climate (leave it to the social workers) or multiplying self-emptying love to the alcoholic and the unwed mother (the Salvation Army's job). Only through involvement do we experience Christian love in its purest form.

Prayer: Father, we are challenged to get involved —to act now! Yet as we pursue reconciliation, encourage us to act through honesty and compassion. Amen.

They're Only Young Once

Children

They should learn first to carry out their religious duties toward their own family and in this way repay their parents and grandparents, for that is what pleases God.

I Tim. 5:4

The two basic needs of a child are to feel wanted and to feel secure. However, the basic problem of parents today is not how to make a child feel loved. In spite of mediocre home conditions (emotionally withdrawn parents, numerically large households, low incomes, etc.), most children generally get the attention, affection, and care they need. I think the basic problem most parents have to contend with in the child-rearing process is how to help the child to become secure in a depersonalized society. Although love as acceptance is a prerequisite for security, affection which neglects to project forward into the larger dimensions of maturity, assumes a not-so-sure-of-itself instability in later years.

Without question, one of the more exciting things about contemporary child psychology is its attempt to get more materials for understanding child behavior out of the textbooks and into commonsense language and workable procedures. Many child psychologists and psychiatrists are beginning to suggest (as a reaction against our puritanical heritage) that the important thing for parents to discover is how a child feels about himself. Up until recently many parents thought it acceptable to program their child's behavior. Yet what they failed to see was that when behavior is restricted too narrowly, a child has a tendency to mature emotionally too late.

In reality a child's attitude toward himself is "where it's at." His feelings about self-worth become a gauge which determines not only his most cherished values, but also whom he chooses as friends and the extent to which he will cooperate with society. So our task here is to help our children and youth to discover and to explore their feelings and attitudes.

We have already examined the value of open and honest feelings as they apply to family relationships. Here, we focus upon the positive attitude toward the expression of human feelings, as opposed to the negative attitude that may be formed in our children when we insist, for example, that it is always bad to be angry or that the touching of one's sex organs is sinful. As a matter of fact children

invariably respond more creatively and affection-
ately to a positive, warm atmosphere at home
(which we as parents should create) where similar
feelings may be shared. By occasionally encour-
aging (our positive Christian examples of love will
help) our children and youth to reexamine their
feelings, we should help them reach a point where
they will become more sensitive to and aware of
their negative feelings like anger, which can be
channeled constructively to release frustrations and
tensions.

One of the essentials of Jesus' message was its
accent on the positive. His media was always (except, for example, when he denounced Pharisaic
hypocrisy, and even that was judgment with a touch
of grace) launched from a motivation to rebuild,
to create anew, to get the world to think positively
together on such issues as justice, peace, brotherhood, parent-child relationships. This way he
pointed to is the only one by which we can attain
a greater knowledge and appreciation of one another, and also know the truth. "If you obey my
teaching you are really my disciples; you will know
the truth, and the truth will make you free" (John
8:31-32).

Prayer: Lord, our children and youth need all the
love and security they can get. Doesn't this require
that we become more sensitive to their needs and
more responsive to their questions? Amen.

Soul Mother

Mother's Day

Charm can be deceptive and beauty doesn't last, but a woman who fears and reverences God shall be greatly praised.

Prov. 31:30

Was Mother Goose ever married? Why didn't the humane society prosecute the farmer's wife for discriminating against three blind mice? Why didn't the old woman in the shoe apply for food stamps? Why didn't Jack Sprat's wife go on a low cholesterol diet? Was Peter Pumpkineater really a male chauvinist?

Many of us have the tendency to glorify our heroes and heroines as long as they stay on film and paper. But bring them into the twentieth century and expose their hang-ups, they become just another "us." When historians look back upon the woman's liberation movement, they will not only applaud its leaders' (I mean Mss.') influence upon women's rights, but perhaps more importantly, they will credit them with having transformed the woman's mentality from the Cinderella-soap-opera fantasia to a like-it-is reality. Conscious dreams and projected wishes are therapeutic, particularly for homemakers, in so far as they momentarily release them from problems and anxieties. They become a threat only when they are allowed to impede the freedom of one's behavior.

In past generations grandmother was not confronted with such emotional stresses. She was not pressured, for instance, to attend a garden or club meeting at two, buy food at the supermarket for the evening meal at three, push the children to finish their lessons by four, prepare dinner at four-thirty, serve dinner at five-thirty, dishes at six-thirty, get the children to bed by seven-thirty, and finally read the evening paper in front of the TV by eight-thirty (if she's lucky).

What women have not entertained these questions: "Am I more than a homemaker? Really, who am I and what is my most important function in life?" "Well," some men reply, "economically speaking, she owns forty percent of America's real estate, fifty percent of its industrial stock, the beneficiary of 80 percent of all life insurance policies, spends 85 percent of America's income, and suggests what should be done with the remaining 15 percent." Others suggest that educationally and politically, she is primarily responsible for the education of her children and exercises a decisive influence in public and national elections. Yet how often do we ask, "What is she, spiritually?"

When the Bible suggests that the perfect woman should embody the faithfulness of a Ruth, the prudence of an Esther, or the dedication of a Mary, most women respond in frustration: "If that be the case, I'll never make it." Yes, it's good to have examples to aim toward, but unless we really begin where we are and where God is willing to meet us, spiritual growth will be a long frustrating experience. Actually, the Bible, a story about human weaknesses made strong through the miracle of love, stresses that authentic spiritual growth is possible through faith (as it responds positively to God's love). And woman, as well as man, has been given a set of tools by her Creator (intellectual powers and creativity, a moral consciousness and spiritual qualities) with which to bring to life God's design in her community, her nation, and her world. Paul teaches that, once she sets her mind and spirit on this priority of discipleship, great things will open up in her life: "But the Spirit produces love, joy, peace, patience, kindness, goodness, faithfulness, humility, and self-control" (Gal. 5:22).

The possibilities for women in the church are quite staggering (and quite frightening for some men in power). As in ages past, they can challenge us men to recycle our wasted energies into renewed homes, turned-on churches, and a more reclaimed society. Right on and amen!

Prayer: Dear God: We thank you for our mothers. Although age may slow their minds and time stammer their voices, may their love and compassion remain an inspiration to us always. Amen.

He's Out to Win You Over This Year

Pentecost

The wind blows wherever it wishes; you hear the sound it makes, but you do not know where it comes from or where it is going. It is the same way with everyone who is born of the Spirit.   John 3:8

There is something intriguing about the appearance of fire. Man, since the primeval ice age, has respected in awe this common phenomenon. Even his understudy, the animal, has kept a respectable distance from its sudden appearance. In substance, fire has a strange way of casting a spell upon its captive audience, be it man or beast. The Santa Ana wind (often called the witch's wind) of California is notorious for its abrupt and deadly surge through the canyon from the northeast spreading fires through the San Gabriel forest and causing property damage around the Los Angeles basin.

Yet we, as creatures of the material world, do not

hold a monopoly on fire. God has toyed with it for various reasons, too. The biblical drama demonstrates this in quite a dramatic way. For fire suggested to biblical man the unfolding of God's Spirit; a Spirit which purifies, heals, and renews. We recall the happening on Mt. Sinai where Jehovah revealed his will to Moses through the burning bush. Later on foreign ground, Baal's territory, Mt. Carmel, he unleashed his Spirit to Elijah by consuming his sacrifice with fire from heaven. Then in the temple he displayed his awesome presence to Isaiah with the burning coal. Beside the river of Chebar he disclosed his divine purpose through the fiery whirlwind from the north. Finally, on the day of Pentecost, the power of his Spirit descended from heaven with a rushing wind and tongues of fire.

So God has made his mark on human history, often with the branding-iron technique, singing the living hell out of men and restoring the power of heaven into his life-style.

The winds of his Spirit are blowing both within the church and amid our secular society today. In spite of the institutional trappings, archaic patterns, and pigeon-hold moralities to which the church has so often confined the majority of its efforts, God's Spirit is still as free and mobile as the wind. The question, then, is not "Where does it originate?" but, "Where will it lead us if we are willing to move on out with it?" Wasn't this God's hardcore message at Pentecost: "Now it's time for you to get with it.

I'll provide the spiritual power if you'll provide the faith power and the man power. Together we'll turn the world upside down!"

Similarly, there is a subterranean happening in the church today. That is to say, many persons are being turned-on by the power of this incredible Spirit. It's changing whole congregations. Prayer and devotional experiences are becoming more relevant where we live, work, and play. Healing is taking place. People are becoming more human. They are discovering God as fresh as the morning. They are becoming liberated from sophisticated titles and status golden calves and being taken in by a more intense celebration of one's being, where joy is the inevitable by-product. In this new fellowship where, potentially, we can be literally electrified by the power of God's Spirit and yet come out alive—totally alive—we will take on the authentic Christ.

Prayer: Lord God, who promised us your presence in the form of the Holy Spirit, continue to monitor that power on the frequency of our faith. Keep us tuned in even though we create static in our witness to others. Amen.

A Triple Threat?

The Trinity

The grace of the Lord Jesus Christ, the love of God, and the fellowship of the Holy Spirit be with you all.

II Cor. 13:13

If you were asked to list the three least understood doctrines of the church, certainly the doctrine of the Holy Trinity would come in a close second or third to the doctrines of Christian eschatology and sanctification. To many the Trinity is about as exciting as Matthew's genealogy and Zephaniah's woes to Moab. The reason for this lack of interest may be attributed to two possible factors. Either the doctrine is too abstract to comprehend (we learn more effectively by identifying with concrete symbols) or, more simply, we have never had it sufficiently explained to us in the first place. It's almost like the triple option in football. You never know who is going to end up with the ball; or, in our case, who is (Father, Son, or Holy Spirit) really doing the addressing. Personally, I have difficulties in explaining it to my congregation. For example,

A Triple Threat?

I always stress that, as water is manifest in three forms (solid, ice—liquid, water—vapor, steam), and its molecular structure isn't changed from one state to another, so it is with the Holy Trinity. God is known as Father, Son, and Holy Spirit. Even this explanation falls short of the real thing.

Ironically, the most complex question the Christian church has wrestled with through the centuries is the nature of God and how we can know him on a more intimate level. Yet after all has been said (explained) and done, the best thing that we have been able to come up with on this count is the Trinity. In spite of its obvious problems ("If Christianity is unified in Spirit, then how come there are three Gods-in-one?"), Samuel Mikoliski says, "The Christian doctrine of the Trinity is indispensable to the Christian understanding of God, salvation, and the divine purpose in creation."

What does all this suggest to us as Christian families? Perhaps, the concept of the Trinity suggests that it is more vital to have an experience *with* God than a casual knowledge *about* God. Few of us would disagree that God does exist. The issue is how real is his existence to us today? If we know Christ on a man-to-Man basis, then we will acquire a more profound glimpse into his Father's nature and a greater grasp of the workings of the power of his Spirit as it permeates (with the grace of love and truth) the many dimensions of human existence. The doctrine of the Trinity also alludes to the fact (or shall we say experience?) that God speaks to us not only through the most powerful forces in the universe, but also through the commonplace relationships which we experience daily. The biblical events that really turned men about-face were those loaded with the sound and the fury of nature's cruelest elements: Job and the whirlwind, Ezekiel and the fiery cloud, Elijah and the earthquake. However, most of us are not Isaiahs and Zechariahs. If God really speaks to us at all, he addresses us most significantly when we least expect it and from the most unlikely of circumstances.

If I had to pinpoint my calling into the ministry, it occurred in a casual outdoor youth retreat where God's will began to permeate my consciousness. It was a gradual (and still continuing) process, certainly not dramatic. God may address us through a wife's smile, the simple touch of a friend, the cry of a hungry child, the grief of a father. Moreover, he communicates his intentions through us to others as well. For if our faith is willing to open itself to the responsibilities and possibilities of his power, we will radiate with this come-on: "My God Isn't dead! In fact he's more alive than you realize!"

Prayer: When new moralities become clichés and when churches compromise with secularism (and then rediscover their souls), we have the assurance that your truth stands forever. Amen.

This Thing Called Love

Marriage

A man leaves his father and mother and is joined
to his wife in such a way that the two become one
person.

Gen. 2:24

The portrait of marriage is becoming so dis-
colored by secular touch-up jobs, that the future
survival of its original beauty, solidarity, and sanc-
tity is questioned. This is to say that many of our
young adults today are beginning to create new
practices of sexuality against the fading backdrop of
puritanical legalism. These activities are observed,
for example, in the dilution of premarital chastity,
the breakdown of inter-marital loyalty, as well as
the acceleration of extra-marital play.

As a direct result, sex is being redirected from
its biblical foundation of authentic love and re-
fashioned into a potentially destructive force. It is
here that sex becomes cheap and void of spiritual
meaning and value. This attempt to isolate sex from

love is evidenced in an increase in pregnancies and venereal disease in our high schools and in so-called free love which falls far short of self-giving concern and responsibility.

Certainly, the Christian religious posture does not write off sex. On the contrary sex is beautiful. And it attains its highest degree of intense meaning within self-giving, responsible, maturing love. In fact the biblical affirmation of marriage suggests that marriage is capable of becoming one of the greatest experiences known to a man and woman. It can become a means toward the end of fulfillment; and through this fulfillment, they can demonstrate to others that religion really works in a day of synthetic new moralities.

Let's be more practical. At which points does love become authentic in the marital dialogue? Love becomes the real thing in a marriage when both husband and wife focus their activities upon *common interests*. These interests, of course, should be represented in everyday activities which we as married couples enjoy doing together. Through the experiences of play, we have an opportunity to reinstate romance in a marriage which may be somewhat on the dud as a result of crying babies and burned roasts. These occasional honeymoons also give us a chance to take stock of our marriage, to talk it out honestly in a romantic atmosphere. We may talk over such questions as, What significant things are lacking in our relationship? Do we worship our children too much? In addition, there are many things we may want to do together: golfing, hiking, camping, or any form of mutual play that becomes a means toward the end of reinforcing our love together.

Love may also become the real thing in marriage when husband and wife attempt to become more *emotionally compatible.* The basic purpose of engagement is not only for discovery, but for mature growth. Marriages must move forward and discover new dimensions such as parenthood. Otherwise, due to a breakdown of communications in our relationship, emotional strife and frustration will result. How many husbands and wives really know each other intimately as human beings? How many really have the capacity to level with one another during a crisis situation?

Consider this formula: love + understanding = compatibility. Christian love strikes a proper balance between two emotional forces, husband and wife. This does not mean a marriage will always be smooth and void of occasional conflict. To the contrary there is therapy in disagreement. How could we test our love without challenge?

Prayer: We strive to stuff our computers with knowledge while our hearts rust from a lack of compassion. Lord, shatter our sophisticated masks and titles that we may respond obediently to the winds of your love. Amen.

Making Love a Family Affair

Love and Morality

This is my commandment: love one another, just as I love you. The greatest love a man can have for his friends is to give his life for them.

John 15:12-13

"Love" is the most remarkable four-letter word in the human language. Yet in its distorted form love is capable of feeding static into the wavelength of human relationships. The complexity of the human personality is such that, as it treats the emotional channels of love, it can manufacture love products under many labels. For example, there is the half-baked love-friends—hate-enemies variety; the yellow-boned I-love-your-Church-O-Lord-as-long-as-it-stays-irrelevant series; or the Fourth-of-July-God-bless-America-and-kill-a-Commie-for-Christ assortment.

However, love in these dimensions ultimately fails to satisfy the in-depth needs of men and women alienated by loneliness and despair. Rather, love, as a potential transforming force in the totality of hu-

74

man relationships, has the power to give structure and unity to personality where it reaches out like a vine and grasps others who, also, seek self-giving relationships.

More significantly, however, love in its purest form is Christian. Christian love is thorough and complete, one which extends its power into every facet of life. Love in this dimension not only has a healing quality about it, but also comes on as a sustaining force throughout the process of Christian growth and maturity.

But isn't Christian love too idealistic? How can we be assured it will work in these times of war, prejudice, and hatred?

Love is for real! It works only when we are willing to turn it on in our lives. History has demonstrated that when love has been properly turned-on man can do his thing by fulfilling his highest potential in the process of reconciliation. Through love the New Testament church found hope in a world of aggressive Roman power; through love St. Francis taught the medieval world the lesson of humility; through love the Protestant Reformation gave the church a new lease to faith and works; despite persecution love implanted an American Dream. Even today in our current social revolution, love is attempting to inject sanity into violence and discrimination.

How, then, does this New Testament breed of love actually function?

Act I: *The Approach*. God makes the first move in this drama of Christian love. As the ultimate Source behind this substance of reconciliation, God approaches man where he is, on his level of moral failure. He is a Father seeking a confused son (Luke 15:11-32), a Shepherd searching for a lost sheep (Matt. 18:10-14).

Act II: *The Response*. If man is perceptive enough to cash in on this love, he is primed to return the favor. Why? By nature man must be constantly programmed by love, he must be reinforced by a self-giving concern which is greater than himself.

Act III: *The Reaction*. This is the climactic act in the total drama of Christian love, namely, man latching onto his brother. This means that, if we honestly love all men, we will attempt to do all that is humanly possible to give them an opportunity to participate in the life of freedom, the liberty for equal opportunity, the pursuit to gain the decent and happy existence.

Thus, we as parents must accept the responsibility to teach our children and youth the nature and the implementation of this love through the choices we make and the relations we have personally with others.

Prayer: Through the power of your love, Lord, give us the grace to be Christ-minded, the strength to be moral, and the faith to be visionary. Amen.

The Child-Rearing-Young-at-Heart Hero

Father's Day

Listen and grow wise, for I speak the truth—
don't turn away. For I, too, was once a son, tenderly
loved by my mother as an only child, and the com-
panion of my father. He told me never to forget
his words.

Prov. 4:1-4

Dad is not as sacred as he once was—or so it
seems at times. His power and authority have been
eroded by "theirs dearly," woman's lib. He's been
called everything from daddy-o to a male chauvinist you-know-what. He's the child's hero and
often the teen's spoilsport. His family expects him
to have the wisdom of Solomon, the courage of
Samson, the patience of Job, and the finesse of a
Roger Staubach in the Sunday afternoon tag football games; while he does well to meet the monthly
budget and take a long-deserved two-weeks' vaca-
tion. Paul Harvey reminds us that "Fathers are what

give daughters away to other men who aren't nearly good enough . . . so they can have grandchildren that are smarter than anybody's."

The role of man as father has indeed reached crisis proportions in many American homes today. Perhaps, the two most serious criticisms leveled against him are that he doesn't communicate too effectively with his wife and that he spends far too much time away from his family. He often postpones his deep affection for and interest in their sons, until adolescence, and then wonders, why he has little or no rapport with the boy or why the son has difficulty in deciding who he is (identity crisis) and what he will choose as a lifetime vocation. By withholding warm affection from his daughter, he may cause an adolescent girl to experience an insecurity and lack of confidence when attempting to relate to young men her own age. Comedian Alan King recently confessed: "It's not easy being a father. But I've been allowed a comeback. The greatest danger is that we see what is happening but we don't want to see it, we don't want to believe it."

Obviously, the solution to this dad-crisis is far too complex to respond to the antiquated start-taking-the-kids-to-church-and-face-up-to-home-responsibilities approach. True, these are vital options to his solution. Yet they fall flat by themselves. What dad needs is not to do more good turns or make more token expressions of love to keep everybody happy in the household—but to develop more effective skills. Paul gives a careful analysis of this point when he stressed to the church at Ephesus: "Parents, do not treat your children in such a way as to make them angry. Instead, raise them with Christian discipline and instruction" (6: 4). Note that he distinguishes, between "treat" (which suggests poorly thought-out action) on the one hand and "raise" (which suggests the technique of common sense and wisdom) on the other. Children and youth do not want to be treated or manipulated like computers; they want and need to be listened to carefully, understood, and reassured. For instance, we as fathers need to sit down with our children and explore, clarify, and work through their fears and suspicions. Otherwise, those fears and suspicions develop into critical hang-ups in the adult world. Many so-termed problem children would never have reached the psychiatrist's office had their fathers (and mothers) made their home atmosphere more receptive to freedom of thought and mutual respect of one's point of view.

Prayer: Although you have endowed mothers with the grace of tenderness, Lord, what we fathers need is a more generous serving of the grace of patience. Amen.

Eden Revisited

God, Nature, and Ecology

Yet there was this hope: that creation itself would one day be set free from its slavery to decay, and share the glorious freedom of the children of God.

Rom. 8:20-21

Recently, I asked an over-sixty congressional assistant to clarify the congressman's position on environmental pollution and he replied: "Well, you know, Americans have gone crazy over ecology" (suggesting, of course, that things aren't as bad as they appear). Evidently, he thought pollution was a necessary evil to be tolerated and lived with the best way possible. Nonsense! If our ancestors had assumed the attitude that all major problems of the human race were insoluble, then human progress would have scarcely advanced beyond what is often referred to as the Neanderthal level.

To be sure, statistics on pollution from the media have so over-conditioned us with a doomsday-or-else picture, that many of us have over-reacted with a what's-use-of-trying-anyhow mentality. Consider these alarming facts on pollution. The Atlantic Ocean is as twice as polluted as it was at the turn of the century; since 1940, the climate of the world has gone into a cooling trend; since 1600, nearly 120 forms of mammals and 225 birds have become extinct, and over 600 forms of animal life face an identical fate in the near future; in the state of North Carolina alone, two million dollars are spent annually on cleaning up litter from the highways. Do these statistics really alarm us, particularly those of us who have children and grandchildren? After all, isn't it they who will have to clean up and pay for our careless exploitation of Mother Earth?

Leo Burnett has called our attention to the priority: "Now is the time for all good men to come to the aid of their planet." And *some* of us are! Most effectively, the government has legislated programs which will drastically reduce automobile emissions and air-land-water pollution. However effective governmental controls and corporation crash programs may be, ultimately, the greatest effort must come from us as individuals.

Before any reclamation of our polluted planet is undertaken, we must first retrace our consideration to one inescapable priority, God. The biblical interpretation of ecology has two focuses: God's ownership and man's stewardship. The psalmist celebrates God as Creator: "The Heavens are telling the glory of God; they are a marvelous display of his crafts-

81

manship" (19:1). God also gives man, a product of his creative hand, a distinctive role to play in his created set up. "And God blessed them and told them, "Multiply and fill the earth and subdue it; you are masters of the fish and birds and all the animals" (Gen. 1:28). Yet mastery does not mean ownership to the point of exploitation. The misuse and careless waste of his material world spells judgment and punishment: "The land suffers for the sins of its people. . . . Therefore, the curse of God is upon them" (Isa. 24:4, 6). But a careful and appreciative use of nature carries with it hope and peace: "At that time I will make a treaty between you and the wild animals. . . . Then you will lie down in peace and safety, unafraid" (Hosea 2:18).

What can be done at home and in the community to combat this problem? (And the real problem is not pollution but polluters.) The problem of environmental pollution will be remedied in direct proportion to the renewal of the human heart and its attitude toward nature. Shortly after our congregation began collecting newspapers for recycling, one lady commented to my wife: "I hadn't thought that saving newspapers would help conserve trees." And that's hope!

Prayer: Father, how we often forget in our technological exploitations that you are Creator. Please keep us humble in our responsibilities both to the world of nature and the world of humanity. Amen.

Is God Down on Softball and Tennis?

Play

Always be joyful in the Lord.

Phil. 4:4

We fathers have a way of evading additional responsibilities, particularly if we're deeply involved in something at the moment. By nature, perhaps, we don't want to be bugged constantly or pressured too hastily into a decision. Thank God, he gave women the unique ability to change their minds on the spur of the moment. Where would human progress be without such incredible decisions?

I recall last summer how my two children kept hinting that I make them a playhouse in the backyard. Of course, I continued to rationalize that it took too much time from my busy schedule (question: who makes our schedules? answer: don't we?), and that it would involve a great deal of expense. Then it dawned on me that, really, building a play house was not such a bad idea after all. Immediately, my mind flashed back to my childhood where we made tree houses along the banks of the Ohio River.

There we were, as carefree as swallows, doing our thing with bent rusty nails and discarded egg cartons (they were made of wood in those days). So I gave in and agreed to build the thing (later I would refer to it as their Peppermint Lounge), but on the condition that they pitch in and do their share, as well.

At that point miracles began to happen. After the foundation had been laid, a neighbor began bringing scrap lumber home from his job, another donated the roofing, while grandparents donated paint as a birthday present to the children. Each evening (make that five out of seven) over a six-weeks period, I would saw wood while Sharyn and Mark would take turns driving nails and cleaning up scraps. My wife, a little more ambitious, did the interior decorating (on paper, of course). And the greatest miracle of all was that this project wasn't work—it was play!

One of the intriguing qualities of the Bible is found in its skillful use of the element of surprise. If you were to read the Bible for the first time ever, you could not possibly anticipate God's next move. So it is with the element of play. The biblical personalities were human, perhaps at times too human for their own good. Yes, they had their tragedies and sufferings, but they had a great time of it, too— and at the most unlikely of places: David, dancing like a love-sick schoolboy before the Ark of the Covenant; Solomon, gunning his chariot down Jerusalem's main drag (with his bumper sticker reading: "With love from the girls of Jerusalem!") Ezekiel, literally eating God's honey-coated words; Jesus, mixing drinks at a wedding party.

If there is any one distinction between biblical times and our secular age, surely it must be found in the fact that we take ourselves far more seriously. This is even evident in our approach to play. Unlike children who can make a dream world out of cardboard boxes and brooms, we adults are more inclined to analyze our play in instant-replay fashion. We worry so much about having a good time that we become fatigued and frustrated even before the game begins. Then we turn to the glass moron to be entertained.

Spontaneous, flexible, unplanned (and sometimes silly) play, actually, is the groove point; it's where it's at! If we spend the remainder of our lives waiting around for exciting things to happen without opening ourselves to the laughter and joy of our children, then we become deteriorated Archie Bunkers—sluggish, narrow, and plain boring. Only by playing and laughing like little children again (as Jesus suggested) will we discover a new self within us full of vigor and joy.

Prayer: Lord of the dance, the trumpet, and the cymbal, excite our minds and bodies with the rhythm of your Spirit. And set our hearts alive to the joyous sounds of nature. Amen.

Blessed Are the Giants, for They Shall Live Longer!

Health

Offer yourselves as a living sacrifice to God, dedicated to his service and pleasing to him.

Rom. 12:1

Generally speaking, most people associate religion with the mind and the soul, not the anatomy of the human body. If there is any one thing unique about the church today, perhaps it may be found in the phenomenon of flabby, tension-prone saints. It's quite a joke on our faith when an overweight minister delivers a sermon on spiritual disciplines. Does this condition alone contribute to the fact that we have fewer great spiritual giants in the church today?

The biblical personalities were anything but weaklings. We often forget that Hebrew men and women lived in a survival-of-the-fittest world with constant exposure to the raw elements. If they didn't work, they didn't eat. To go on welfare would have been more preposterous than Noah's attempting to build an ark on dry land. Yet some of the greatest men and writings of history have come out of this type of primitive environment. It could well be that God speaks most clearly to those who are exposed daily to the crude forces of nature and who survive with strength: Amos, a herdsman; Job, a prosperous rancher; Peter, a fisherman.

Moreover, God does not confine his monitoring system to biblical characters alone. He has gotten in his good Word throughout the history of the church —that is, to those who would listen. Consider the example of John Wesley in eighteenth-century England. He put his feet where his religion was, walking miles daily for physical exercise. In comparison with contemporary standards and programs of physical fitness, Wesley had a good thing going. It was a thorough and demanding plan, applicable to us today. He outlines these guidelines necessary for a more healthy anatomy and a trim physical frame.

1. *Exercise.* He writes in his Journal: "Use as much exercise daily in the open-air as you can without weariness. Walking is the best exercise. . . . We may strengthen any weak part of the body by constant exercise." Beginning gradually, we should adopt a regular schedule of exercise whether it be twice weekly at the Y or more informally, walking or jogging in the mornings or evenings.

2. *Eating Habits.* "Use plain diet, easy of digestion, and this as sparingly as you can. . . . Eat very light, if any, supper." It is not only important what we eat of nutritional value (watch the mayonnaise

at lunch), but how much we eat, as well (fewer TV snacks, Dad).

3. *Cleanliness.* "Everyone that would preserve health should be as clean and sweet as possible in their houses, clothes and furniture." This cleanliness-next-to-Godliness approach has a great deal of common sense attached to it. We all know how viruses, created by unsanitary conditions, can almost cripple us overnight.

4. *Sleeping Habits.* "Sleep early and rise early, never lie in bed much above seven hours." Either too much or too little sleep is capable of keeping the mind drowsy and sluggish.

5. *The Psychosomatic Factor.* "Beware of anger, beware of worldly sorrow, beware of fear that hath torment, beware of foolish and hurtful desires, beware of inordinate affection." These negative attitudes only lead to adverse affects upon the physical body such as ulcers and nervousness. To the contrary, this is one of the reasons why Jesus' formula of love and faith really works. I don't think it unreasonable to suggest that those who love authentically and act accordingly, actually live longer. Which, really, is more important, our lives or our pride?

Prayer: We thank you for our biological frames, Father. Through proper care and exercise, help us to make it into a temple worthy of your Spirit. Amen.

The Joy Happening

Happiness

Happy are the pure in heart: they will see God!

Matt. 5:8

An English newspaper recently asked: "Who are the happiest people on earth?" The reply was: a craftsman whistling over a job well done; a child building a sand castle; a mother bathing her baby; a physician finishing a difficult operation to save a human life. It is interesting to note that two of these examples involve the family, while the other two involve men, possibly fathers, busy making other people happy. I think this demonstrates that most of the happiness (such as emotional security, spiritual fulfillment, and joy) in today's world exists among parents and children and youth and other relatives. This argument in itself is enough to dispute the claim that the family unit as we know it is on the way out.

Within the past decade there has been a gigantic invasion of self-help family-life books on the market. These proposals have provided an invaluable source of help and hope for many contemporary families. And strangely enough, it seems as if the ones written from the practical perspective of "I don't have all the answers, but I'll be honest about my personal knowledge and experience," have become the highly successful ones. Still, one of the bewildering things about so many books on happiness is the problem, which one?

In any case, I think it is helpful for us occasionally to revaluate the meaning of happiness in our homes and the shape it is taking in our varied relationships as a family. Let us consider the following guidelines which may help us to keep the significance of family happiness constantly before us.

1. *It's love that makes the world* (at home, at least) *go round*. Perhaps too much emphasis has been placed on this quality in family relationships, but, in reality, it's the golden cord that keeps the home together. Obviously, too much love leads to the over-protection of our children, while too little love leads to insecurity and a lack of confidence. Being as impartial as possible with our attention to our children, temperate and reasonable in our discipline, and consistent in warm affection is the name of the game.

2. *Don't cop out from the human scene.* Reassurance of our children more through praise for what they are as human beings than for what they do as members of a household should not be forgotten. Don't expect perfection from them. Far too many parents expect perfection from their children,

when all the while the children can see through their parents and discover their imperfections and weaknesses in disguise.

3. *Born free?* Although we all aim toward family togetherness, let's not forget that we all must grow as independent individuals, too. As we encourage our children to make independent decisions, we must avoid nagging or criticizing them for making occasional wrong choices. Help them to see at which point the choice was off-center and let them take it from there without further interference.

4. *Hard work never hurt anyone!* Parents who give their children and youth everything may ultimately discover that their sons and daughters will return little in the way of respect and true affection. The drug scene with its run-away youth is testimony to this affluent giveaway. Children and youth want to work, to be responsible, to experience achievement in a job well done around the house and in the yard.

5. *Spiritual exercises.* Teaching our children to love God and to practice that love in all of life's decisions and activities gives them a faith and strength they will always draw from—even when they become parents.

Prayer: Dear God, we need the happiness which only your Spirit can give, the kind that's grounded in your love, the kind that helps us to live at peace both with ourselves and with others. Amen.

Spiritual Go-Power

Discipleship

If anyone wants to come with me, he must forget
himself, carry his cross, and follow me.

Matt. 16:24

In *The Wizard of Oz,* there is a personality one
could hardly forget, the cowardly lion. His hang-
up was fear. As a result of this attitude, he was incapable of attaining his self-identity, his rightful
role as a lion. Such a moral posture is not sheer
fantasy because many of us who claim the title
Christian, remain in our little shells of fear whenever it comes to flexing our moral muscles. We are
fearful that, if we display our moral attitudes daily,
we may be given the axe by our friends. However,
we not only betray ourselves, but we fail others who
might be influenced by our moral position.

What form, then, should our discipleship, our
allegiance to Christ, take? One thing is certain;
it cannot be confined to a neatly packaged bag of
tricks from which we may meet life's hurtful habits

with helpful hints from on high! Jesus did not buy starchy legalisms and matchbox moralities. He did not come to the world to destroy but to create and to fill with meaning. As a result of his new lease on life, he programmed the Judaic law with love, responsibility, and freedom. He gave it purposive direction. For the first time in human history, he gave morality authentic life which resounded with meaning! " 'You must love the Lord your God with all your heart, and with all your soul, and with all your mind.' This is the greatest and the most important commandment. The second most important commandment is like it: 'You must love your neighbor as yourself' " (Matt. 22:37-40).

Luke's portrayal of Zacchaeus, the Tom Thumb disciple, provides us with one of the more remarkable stories of the effect of Jesus' gospel of love and responsibility on the human personality. We know nothing of the tax collector's prior experience with Jesus. Evidently, he was interested enough that, once when Jesus was passing through Jericho, he climbed a tree to see what the young man from Nazareth had to say. And when Jesus passed below he shocked the daylights out of Zacchaeus, by saying: "Hurry down, Zacchaeus, for I must stay in your house today." Still in a daze, the little man descended and enthusiastically took Jesus up on the offer.

So Zacchaeus was changed dramatically. More than that, he put his money where his heart was by confessing to Jesus: "Listen, sir! I will give half my belongings to the poor; and if I have cheated anyone, I will pay him back four times as much." Jesus said to him, "Salvation has come to this house today" (Luke 19:8-9).

In contrasting Zacchaeus with the rich young man, we can observe that the little disciple was willing to risk his cozy securities, his stocks and bonds, for a pulsating life of joy and fulfillment. And Jesus' confidence was restored, in some rich men who could enter heaven through the eye of a needle after all!

One of Stan Freberg's "God Commercials" of the last decade summarizes this Jesus-Zacchaeus episode:

> Where'd you get the idea
> You could make it all by yourself?
> Doesn't it get a little lonely sometimes,
> Out on a limb . . . without Him . . . ?
> It's a great life, but it could be greater,
> Why try and go it alone?
> The blessings you lose may be your own.

How about us?

Prayer: Discipleship means meeting you halfway with a committed faith, Father. Therefore, help us to try again when we have failed miserably; to do our best when we have experienced our worst. Amen.

Emerge and Become

Family Worship

God is Spirit, and those who worship him must worship in spirit and in truth.

John 4:24

We are all aware of a decrease of attendance in our American churches, and it would not be difficult to penetrate the source of the problem: the deterioration of family unity. Yet, whenever a family directly participates in a worship experience on Sunday morning (keeping in mind, of course, that the service is reasonably contemporary and relevant), it becomes more involved in the total life of the church itself. Here is how it works: If our children are taught to listen carefully to the sermon (if it's not over twenty-five minutes), to understand what they are singing in the hymns (if the language isn't over one hundred years old), to share their allowances during the offering, they become more concerned with the authentic purpose and function of the church in our society today. They may even become absorbed in Christian fellowship and community service projects.

In addition to corporate worship, families must worship privately and regularly. In a sense, this kind of worship can become most influential in molding the moral character of the family. Obviously, worship in the home entails much more than reading irrelevant Bible selections from I Chronicles, followed by a nice harmless thought and a three-sentence prayer in King James verse. Certainly, good devotional literature is capable of functioning as a springboard to a more hardcore sharing of family problems and other experiences. This is what is lacking in many Christian families today. Members do not really know one another on an intimate level. They find it difficult to relate. As a result a communications gap is forged.

In our homes we will find it more meaningful and helpful if we begin to share our daily experiences (fragrant or bittersweet) after dinner in an informal setting (perhaps out in the backyard or even sitting on the livingroom floor). As strange as it may appear, such an approach to family sharing can become a moment for healing those broken relationships and rekindling warm affection. Husband and wife relationships can become more open and honest, and we may rediscover our children as authentic human beings capable of exciting joy and fulfillment.

Many of us may want to rationalize that this

approach to private family worship is a great deal of trouble. Is it really worth all this effort? Actually, worship experiences centered in such a sharing technique build enduring trust and love as acceptance (we care about one another's problems). But there is more in this in-depth openness. We also grow and mature creatively. And only then are we capable of coping as a family with such inevitable red-light situations as shaky adolescence, checkbook blues, tinkertoy moralities, and, well, we know what else.

We as Christian families should finally conclude our interpersonal devotional encounter with a brief prayer asking God to make his love a more dominant theme in our lives and to strengthen our willingness to work through our problems together. As Christians we believe in the potential power force of prayer as a reliable source of strength (not as a selfish gimmick to bribe God's services)—a spiritual reality we can rely on when all other options have been exhausted.

Prayer: If we phase out the home from our secular life-style, Lord, then where else can we turn for security, peace of mind, acceptance? Shouldn't we focus our worship experiences around these themes? Amen.

The Jesus People

Who Is Jesus?

I tell you the truth: I am the door for the sheep . . . .
I have come in order that they might have life,
life in all its fulness.

John 10:7, 10

Whenever the American Dream is interrupted by the nightmare of war, crime, and a general unrest, our minds have a tendency to become psyched by nostalgia, and we attempt to relive the "good old days" (whatever that means). Today, nostalgia is in, and Buffalo Bob, (whatever happened to Princess Summerfallwinterspring?), and Superman are making a strong comeback. Yet, of all the nostalgic personalities to be resurrected, a figure named Jesus is the most interesting and intriguing by far. And what makes him so fascinating is not what he did, but who he was. These anonymous lines from "One Solitary Life" describe his utter simplicity and humility:

> He was born in an obscure village, the child of a
> peasant woman. He worked in a carpenter shop until

he was 30. Then for three years he was an itinerant
preacher. He never wrote a book. He never held an
office. He never had a family or owned a house.
He never went to college. He never traveled 200
miles from the place where he was born.

He never did one of the things that usually accompany
greatness. He had no credentials but himself.

Personally, I am convinced that one of the reasons Jesus has captured the attention of thousands of today's youth is that they never really knew the man before—ever. And I think that we may go so far as to say that, even though most of these youth have gone to Sunday school and church all their lives, the only picture they received of him was a pious, sugary, frowning, semifeminine, harmless hybrid of a human being. Then some of us wonder why they have become turned-off by the institutional church.

Hopefully, all that is behind us. Again, however, we must reconsider the question: "Who is Jesus as a person?" For starters, he was a gregarious individual, one who loved people and who loved life itself. He went to the people where they were and confronted their needs with a lingo and idiom they could all understand and identify with. When the occasion called for it, he could be understanding and compassionate or even firm and courageous in the face of injustice. As a thoroughbred human being he could smell the salt on the Sea of Galilee, touch the petals on a desert flower, taste the dust on

Judean roads, experience the beaded brow in his father's carpenter shop.

Then, too, there was a most unique twist about his personality, he was God, too. Whenever he confronted a man or woman with the faith option, he didn't come across with preachy shoptalk. He didn't bore with trivialities. Yes, he would rap awhile informally to loosen you up. Then he would hit you with his truth, treating humility/pride, benevolence/greed, marriage/divorce, love/hate, death /eternal life, sin/salvation. And before you would know it, he would have you in the palm of his hand. You would never forget him—nor he you.

Jesus, the man, the Son of God, teacher, prophet, pastor, miracle-worker, reconciler of social injustices, is still in circulation. He's on the scene with the same credentials monitoring the same Good News about how great it is to be alive and how we can bring a war-worn, sin-sickened, drug-disgusted humanity to life with hope and love. And if we have the courage to admit that we know him, then others will surely discover him through us. What an incredible opportunity for the Christian family.

Prayer: It is generally assumed that seeing is believing. Isn't it also true that unless we believe in you, we will be unable to see you? If this is our problem, Jesus, set us straight with your truth. Amen.

Sweat It Out for God's Sake!

Labor Day

What matters is to obey God's commandments.
Every man should remain as he was when he accepted God's call.

I Cor. 7:19-20

Jesus was never idle or unemployed. He was always occupied with something or someone. He was
more than a man on the go—he was also a man of
action. That was why he was always saying: "My
Father works always, and I too must work" (John
5:17). We recall at this point his occupation in
his carpenter shop before launching his public ministry. Certainly, his work as a craftsman contributed
to his understanding of human nature and his ac-
companying genius to redeem it. This craftsman-
turned-teacher was aware that hard work was both
a gift and an invaluable asset from God. Regarding
the angle of health in vocational work, Jesus once
suggested: "To have good fruit you must have a
healthy tree; if you have a poor tree you will have

bad fruit. For a tree is known by the kind of fruit it bears" (Matt. 12:33). Even his parables and teachings reflect man at work: laborers in a vineyard, a contractor constructing a house, fishermen having difficulty with their nets.

More significantly, however, Jesus gave an additional responsibility to the Christian workman: "The man to whom much is given, of him much is required; the man to whom more is given, of him much more is required" (Luke 12:48). Some of us are naturally more gifted than others. And from those of us who are greatly endowed with initiative and intellectual know-how and who command responsibility in important positions, God will require a great deal. He will expect us to get his job done particularly where the action is.

What a great country we have in America! In spite of occasional radicals who complain about the fallacies of our democratic system, America still remains a country of hope—a nation of unlimited opportunities for all who are willing to make the necessary sacrifice through education and apprenticeship. A life without hard work and initiative is one which goes soft through inactivity and uninvolvement.

There is more that we could enumerate about the values and possibilities of work in our society such as its effect upon the health of our minds and physical bodies. One vital question, however, often remains unanswered: How does the concept and activity of work (or a lack of it) influence the lives of our children and youth?

One could easily begin with attitudes toward work. In what ways do our attitudes influence those of our children and youth? Procastinating and attempting to get by with as little effort as possible in our work may have a great deal to say about our children's Mom-do-I-have-to approach to simple household chores. At a very young age, responsibilities should be delegated to our children such as washing dishes and working in the family garden. I know in our home it is frustrating at times when our children fail to wash the car efficiently according to our expectations. But, really, who cares? Let the car go half-washed. Which is more important: the status image we must set before our neighbors or our children's understanding of an accomplishment of a worthwhile goal and an important contribution to the family? At least in our place, we'll go with the latter.

Prayer: Lord, many of us over forty have been bitten by "suburbanitus" or complacency. Yet doesn't this affect our youth? Lord, we need a home work ethic which balances fulfillment with a sense of accomplishment. Amen.

The Headache File

Family Problems

I consider that what we suffer at this present time
cannot be compared at all with the glory that is
going to be revealed to us.

Rom. 8:18

Perhaps, the most feasible way to handle a meditation like this is to outline briefly the typical problems we face at home and treat them with four or
five surething, experience-tested remedies. I hope to
spare you that frustration. Personally, I've always
been somewhat suspicious of stereotyped, clear-cut
solutions to any problem or issue, for all the solutions do not work for all the people even some of
the time. Keith Miller makes this point when he
states that Jesus wasn't always consistent in his
own life. For example, on one occasion he deplored
violence (Matt. 5:39), while on another drove mer-
chants out of the temple (Matt. 21:12). Miller
says: "Jesus was not consistent with regard to a set
of rules. . . . To be obedient to the perspective of

His Father in new situations, Jesus transcended the old rules. He tried to bring God's vulnerable but healing love to each situation in a way that brought wholeness to the people involved" (*A Second Touch* [Waco: Word Books, 1967], p. 53).

There is a distinction to be made between pat answers (the Law) and guidelines (the gospel of flexible self-emptying love) in that the latter requires a good deal more thought and responsible action.

Our concern, then, is not centered on solutions to our problems, but on the problems themselves. Knowing how to avoid problems is more effective (and less painful) than solutions we must struggle for after our problems have been created. More importantly, knowing the why's to our problems opens up preventive solutions. The fear of our problems and the suffering they inflict will cease to become a dominant theme as before—though we never evade our problems altogether. For there are some problems such as chronic diseases that we must accept as virtually insoluble, and we must attempt to live with them in faith and courage.

How do problems arise in the first place? Most problems seem to appear when we least expect them. And the problems which get out of hand are generally created in one of the following ways. (a) We fail to accept love and to love in return. Authentic love and friendship are threats to the inner self. They are capable of making us new persons, and some of us frankly don't want that. (b) Problems not only arise from attempts to escape the self, but also from the evasion of reality itself. We become frustrated with ourselves and bored sick with business associates. The bottle and the pill are the escape hatch. (c) Immature attitudes frozen in tradition and complacency constitute still another source of human woes. We avoid pain as a threat to our inclusive security and hope to make the transition into eternity in a foam rubber casket. (d) Problems may also emerge in our lives precisely because we give up too easily. This may be further traced to our failure to latch onto the right grade of priorities. Blowing investments, which should be in long-term life insurance, on bigger houses and flashier cars can drastically affect a home whose father becomes disabled.

Too often many of us approach our problems from a negative slant and fail to discover what positive qualities we have going for us. I think the key to the problem-solving process may be found in those qualities all of us are capable of developing: The technique of remaining a few steps ahead of our problems by pinpointing the source in the early stages, remaining as flexible and tolerant as possible under pressure, channeling our drives into constructive areas, maintaining a trust in the power of God's love.

Prayer: Father, would the problems of the world really exist if our difficulties were settled at home? Give us the insight to deal constructively with our problems before they become too complicated. Amen.

Babel's Leaning Tower?

The Church

It was more than we could have hoped for! First they gave themselves to the Lord; and then, by God's will, they gave themselves to us as well.

II Cor. 8:5

As parents seeking to find a more meaningful faith in our homes and at our places of work, we have become deeply concerned about the existing church and what it should be doing in our society. We acknowledge that recent signs of hope are emerging such as a toning-down of impersonalism in the church's organizational apparatus and a rebirth of the dynamics of the Holy Spirit in its group activity.

However, amid the current controversy over the role of faith in social action, we often become confused regarding the strategic direction our church should be taking. After all, the spiritual destiny of our children and grandchildren will be affected by the extent to which the church will shape the future. What is the primary function of the church?

For one thing the true Christian Church exists as *proclamation,* the monitoring of God's Word to men (Matt. 28:19-20). The church at this point must demonstrate the reality of its message by coming through with what it proposes in pulpit statements and church school literature. It must seek to accomplish this through a thrust toward relevance in worship and, a willingness to accept its shortcomings by submitting to a thorough spiritual tune-up in its life. Could a lack of such soul-searching contribute to the fact that many young adults are disengaging themselves from an active participation in the church today?

Another significant task of the true Christian church is that of *fellowship,* the living witness of God's Word among men (I John 1:3-4). This becomes a nucleus of the committed who absorb God's Word and share it in love. Certainly, the plea for community is a desperate cry in our age. The great shifts in population into congested urban areas, the rapid implementation of technology in virtually all life patterns, the manipulation of personal dignity in the interest of political and economic power forces, all combine to shatter man into a litter of fragmented splinters. However, through the unifying power of God's love, the true church as fellowship is capable of reconstructing man's brokenness and emptiness into purposive direction.

A third understanding of the true Christian church is fulfilled through *reconciliation,* the service of God's Word to all men (II Cor. 5:17-18). Never has the church had a greater opportunity to direct man toward inner renewal and reconciliation than our church at this point in the twentieth century! If our church intends to confront the "now" issues with the attitude that we can and will succeed, then we should begin. There is a need for group therapy to unwed mothers, rehabilitation efforts with the alcoholic, unified responses to disaster appeals. Local family task forces could be formed for these ministries. For the church of Jesus Christ represents the only hope for authentic and lasting reconciliation in this generation.

It is precisely within the framework of God's power force that we as Christian families will exercise one of two options. Either as complacent members of a respectable well-to-do church we will continue to duplicate the often humdrum religiosity of the previous generation; or as dedicated men and women we will awaken to the clamor of those issues which engage our brothers, rub our drowsy eyes to see that things are achangin' fast, roll up our clean, starched sleeves, loosen our Sunday ties, and get in step with the week-day citizen on the crowded streets and in the forgotten alleys where his cry for love and community is voiced.

Prayer: Father God, although our technological society meets our wants, it does not always fulfill our basic needs. Help us to see that the church is essentially a "needs" institution. Amen.

Reason or Perish

World Order

They will beat their swords into plowshares and their spears into pruning-hooks; nations shall no longer fight each other, for all war will end.

Micah 4:3

Of all the significant assets attributed to human nature, the one often overlooked is the short memory. Take, for example, the problem of war. It looks as if by now man would have learned that war accomplishes little except death and destruction. Man doesn't always remember that, does he? But if man is so creative and progressive, so enlightened and rational, it looks as if he would have come up with an alternative for settling tribal and national conflicts. In 1951 the late General Douglas MacArthur warned a joint session of Congress:

> Military alliances, balance of powers, leagues
> of nations, all in turn failed, leaving the only
> path to be by the way of the crucible of war. The
> utter destructiveness of war now blocks out this

alternative. We have had our last chance. If we
will not devise some greater and more equitable
system, Armageddon will be at our door.

"Big deal," we say. Well, could the solution be
found in man himself? Are we so naïve as to believe
that wars may be dissolved through the individual?
Well, Jesus did! Big deal? Yet isn't this our problem?
Most of us couldn't recognize a big deal if we saw
one? You see, Jesus made a big deal out of peace;
even to the point that he sacrificed his life for it.
His revolutionary teachings on peace so influenced
the writer of Hebrews, that he wrote: "Try to be
at peace with all men, and try to live a holy life,
for no one will see the Lord without it" (12:14).

I think our problem as parents is that we have
become so conditioned in the past by the fact that
peace is achieved only at the expense of war, that,
frankly, many of us have hang-ups and doubts
about solving our differences (international or personal) in a rational and diplomatic manner. We are
willing to pay our taxes and send our sons to the
battlefield as necessary sacrifices (so we think) to
achieve peace. But it becomes a different ball game
when we have to teach our sons and daughters that
the most important priority we can absorb as a citizen is peace. We are incapable of teaching our children about peace in general, primarily because we
have failed to secure peace in particular, in our marriages and in our attitudes and philosophies of
child-raising. Until our hearts are changed from

violence to peace, hatred to love, we really have no right to criticize politicians for blundering peace efforts when our efforts at home are on the warpath.

Peace also becomes more realistic and achievable when our love-oriented peace at home materializes into justice in our society. A society which produces equality for all in jobs, housing, and education certainly will merit God's approval. This was the bug which Amos uncovered in the Kingdom of Israel. He suggested that by exploiting the poor (a denial of individual peace and freedom), Israel would seal its own doom. Before it was too late, he attempted to call their attention to the handwriting on the wall: "I want to see a mighty flood of justice— a torrent of doing good" (5:24). The question to us is, "Will we?"

My five-year-old son, Mark, recently asked. "Why is Vietnam always on the radio?" I found it difficult to give him an adequate answer. My real desire was to become more Christlike to my son, so I gave him in substance Christ's words: "Happy are those who work for peace among men: God will call them his sons!" (Matt. 5:9)

Prayer: Dear God, through our examples as parents, may we teach our children and youth to employ love in the complex decisions they will make. May they also maintain a faith which believes that the world can live in peace. Amen.

An Open Letter to God

Youth

See how much the Father has loved us! His love is so great that we are called God's children—and so, in fact, we are.

I John 3:1

Dear God:

How much truth is there to Socrates' assessment of our youth?

> They have bad manners, contempt for authority, they show disrespect for adults and love to talk rather than work or exercise. They no longer rise when adults enter the room. They contradict their parents, chatter in front of company, gobble down food at the table, and intimidate their teachers.

Is it entirely applicable for today? Are our criticisms of their appearance and actions really justified? Or is this generation tension actually created on our side of the spectrum? Could the real problem be our failure to listen? Do we fail to listen because we think that we have copyright privileges to the truth? Are we afraid of listening because we are fearful that what they are saying is closer to the truth than we think?

Youth is saying, "Look at me! I exist! I'm for real! What do you see? Long hair, bare feet, and patched jeans? Isn't that at least better than being a slave to status games, shallow securities, and material trinkets?"

To be honest, Lord, for better or for worse, we parents must admit one thing; they're ours! They're the product of our dreams, our homes, our schools, our churches—even our narrow-minded blunders. Could it also be that they simply don't fit the mold (the Depression, postwar expectations) we have placed before them? Could it be that they don't groove on a system of values which delivers little more than a stinking environment and a perfume-scented racism?

Times are changing, though. We both are beginning to observe that no generation has ever been a picture-perfect Eden devoid of human misery and alienation. In reply to Ezekiel's question, "Are children punished for their father's sins?" we both are beginning to answer, "No way—that is, if there's forgiveness, mutual acceptance, and trust." At that point we begin to work it out together.

Isn't that the key to it all? Unless we patiently work together, we labor in vain? For unless we work through the existing political, economic, social, and religious structures of our society (as corrupt and inefficient as they are at times), we will continue to alienate those persons and groups who, with a little time and education (of the wisdom variety), could eventually understand our motivations and get with it, too.

Meanwhile, Lord, we parents have the greater responsibility. With the reservoir of our wisdom and experience, we must open our honest selves to our youth and touch the nerve of their aspirations.

And another thing, Lord, we parents are going to have to be ourselves and remain loyal to a set of moral standards. Our youth desperately need a changeless foundation against which to measure their own lives and launch the critical decisions they will have to make. For they challenge us to break the sounds of silence by letting the sunshine of your love into our life-style. Do we have what it takes to come through on that score? Yet what kind of future does the human race have without your love?

Thanks for listening.

Sincerely,

A frustrated but hopeful parent

Prayer: Forgive us, O God, for thinking we are always right when we are on occasion wrong. Pardon us for dreaming our adult fantasies and neglecting the burning questions of our children and youth. Amen.

The Jesus Revolution

Reformation

For the gospel reveals how God puts men right with himself: it is through faith alone, from beginning to end. As the scripture says, "He who is put right with God through faith shall live."

Rom. 1:17

The Jesus Revolution is certainly not a unique happening in our time. In fact, the church has gotten by from century to century as a result of other such happenings, which emerged and ignited cold cathedrals and deteriorating societies with the flame of renewal. And those who stirred the warm coals of spiritual rebirth were labeled as the equivalent of our "Jesus Freaks" or as something more unmentionable. They pricked the stained-glass bubble of the ecclesiastical establishment and, of course, things were never quite the same again. Why were they tagged as squares? Because they zeroed in with a common theme: get Jesus back into the bloodstream of mother church. Either get a spiritual transfusion or you may have a corpse on your hands. Francis, Luther, Wycliff, Wesley were categorized as odd because they stressed that the faith of their fathers was no longer functional. They proclaimed, "The time has arrived to come up with a new faith of your own in a new age."

When you get down to it, the most exciting thing about spiritual rebirth in the contemporary church is its emphasis upon a renewal of Jesus in its lifestyle. That is even taking priority over budget blues and ham suppers in many churches today. The point the reformers are trying to pass on to us is that only when Jesus' Spirit is in charge of things in the local church, will people be turned *inside out* and *on*. The problem is that when that happens, change— big change—is inevitable. And that turns most of us off because it is too challenging and often too risky for our own comfort.

This Jesus-ferment-spiritual-social-change principle is one which requires further attention. The church, perhaps more than any other institution in our society, has the potential to become a *change agent*. Through its relevant programs and message of proclamation, it can teach us how to accept change as gracefully as possible, to live with it, and to shape it in the direction of purpose and meaning for those who wish to move with it in the future.

Further, the Protestant reformers leave the legacy to us parents that with the Spirit of Jesus, we've got a good thing going. To be sure we can't fully appreciate how good we really have it. There have been moments in the history of the church when parents didn't have the freedom to read Scripture to their children or even have a church to worship in together. Now, when that freedom is offered in unlimited quantities, most of us misuse it for self-interests. If Protestantism has no other point to make about its heritage, it makes this perfectly clear: "Remember! Don't be the first generation since Pentecost to cop out on the celebration of God's Spirit in your lives." Let's be honest with ourselves, where would our homes be in the secular jungle without the influence of his Spirit upon our lives? "But the Spirit produces love, joy, peace, patience, kindness, goodness, faithfulness, humility, and self-control. . . . The Spirit has given us life" (Gal. 5:22, 25).

Prayer: Jesus Christ, Superstar, how we wonder who you are? Does that title seem a bit too secular? But, then, haven't we kept you in stained glass for much too long? Come, Jesus, and excite us with hope. Amen.

Don't Be a Human Dropout

Alcohol

So then, let us stop judging one another. Instead, this is what you should decide: not to do anything that would make your brother stumble, or fall into sin.

Rom. 14:13

The facts on alcoholic abuse are familiar to us all: that over a quarter million new alcoholics become evident each year; that alcoholism ranks fourth as a public health menace behind heart disease, mental illness, and cancer; that it is responsible for over 50,000 highway fatalities annually; that the average death rate for alcoholics is nearly two and one-half times that of the entire population. John L. Norris, a world authority on alcoholism says: "If anything else in the United States created as much tragedy, as many deaths, as does alcoholism, it would have already been declared a national emergency."

So we have a problem. However, what are we going to do about it? Due to the complexity of the problem and the shades of difference in human personalities, alcoholism cannot be remedied in a stereotyped, cut-and-dried manner. Although curative techniques are employed (like Alcoholics Anonymous, medical treatment), if the problem is to be brought under control for the next generation, it must be attacked from a preventative slant, a moral standpoint. The Christian parent, particularly, should consider these suggestions.

First, the parent who insists on drinking must consider the principle of Christian freedom. Paul writes: "For a slave who has been called by the Lord is the Lord's free man; in the same way a free man who has been called by Christ is his slave" (I Cor. 7:22). With this gift of freedom we are called upon in various moral situations to exercise options and choices. And our experience, discipline, and wisdom will be of great assistance at this point. Yet our freedom does not give us a license to do as we please. Again, Paul qualifies this when he writes: "But do not let this freedom become an excuse for letting your physical desires rule you. Instead, let love make you serve one another" (Gal. 5:13).

Ultimately, Christian freedom involves a responsibility, a responsibility to *God* to become a living sacrifice, holy and acceptable to him; a responsibility to *others* to be our brother's keeper; a responsibility *to ourselves* to be temples of the Holy Spirit.

Second, the parent who insists on drinking must consider the principle of a Christian witness. In Romans Paul writes: "This is what you should decide: not to do anything that would make your brother stumble, or fall into sin" (14:13). The implication at this point is if we drink before someone who thinks, drinking is harmful, although in good conscience we think it isn't, there's still the possibility the other person's Christian freedom will be violated. In short, we may be a stumbling block even though our intentions are good.

Also, consider the impact of drinking before children and youth who haven't had the opportunity to explore the issue objectively and morally. Is it fair to run the risk of giving them the wrong impression about drinking—even though you believe you are dead right? Can you really manifest the love of Christ in your drinking? That, to be sure, is a difficult question to resolve.

So the Christian is virtually overwhelmed by responsibilities in a secular age. He must seek the facts and explore thoroughly the issues at hand. He must be honest with others, yet maintain an honesty which reflects self-giving love. And he must employ the tools his Creator gave him: mind, abilities, and creative efforts for God's glory and human enlightenment.

Prayer: Lord, when our youth take drugs and booze, doesn't it indicate that we may have neglected their searching needs during childhood? If so, and if it isn't too late, awaken us. Amen.

Pilgrims in Secular City

Thanksgiving

Go through his open gates with great thanksgiving;
enter his courts with praise.
Give thanks to him and bless his name.

Ps. 100:4

Is Thanksgiving in trouble? Will the celebration
of the harvest festival suffer the same fate as prayer
in public schools? There are some who would de-
lete the national observance of this religious holiday
from our calendar on the grounds that it violates
the concept of the separation of church and state.
It would appear as if many of our national leaders
and legislators have failed to do their homework.
They have neglected to retrace the greatness of our
nation to its primary source: the Constitution and
the Bill of Rights are further established on the
principles of the Christian religion. It is Hebrew history which warns that national arrogance plus spiritual arrogance equal social decadence.

There is a further tragedy to this Thanksgiving

affair. We not only make conscious efforts to omit Thanksgiving as a national holiday, but even worse, we have forgotten the Source of it all: God himself. Robert Louis Stevenson once remarked: "The man who forgets to give thanks is the man who has fallen asleep in life." Evidently, millions of Americans have lost an appreciative perception of life itself. So confined to their little worlds of home and office, their physical senses become blinded and deafened to the dance of the jonquil in the March sunshine, or the celebration of new life in the cry of a new-born child. Undermined by greed and apathy, these persons, dead both to themselves and to God, really sustain little purpose in life. Consequently, their children grow up failing to remember their parents at worship or at prayer expressing a deep-rooted gratitude to God for the gifts of life and happiness. One would have good reason to conclude, then, that the current drug crisis among our youth may in part be traced to attitudes of ingratitude which they inherited from the personalities of their parents.

While their attitudes and personalities are being formed, how may we as parents teach our children the art of perpetual gratitude? As previously indicated, this learning process must begin with our own attitudes and practices of worship. Our family devotions at home should have less of a shallow atmosphere about them and center more upon God as Creator-Giver and our feedback through the expressions of thankful praise. At the same time we may think that we aren't getting through to our children during these sharing moments. But more than we realize, they will remember and cherish the fact that (1) we did things together and (2) we cared enough to let God in on it.

Another possible way we may impress upon our children the value of gratitude is to show them how to give themselves to others. The greater our blessing from God, the greater our responsibility toward those in need. Too often we knock the Thanksgiving-basket morality as a tranquilizer for the conscience. Without question, this has some merit. Yet what these critics fail to understand is that many of the recipients of our material sharing appreciate our sincere intentions more than the gifts themselves. When we take our children and youth into the homes of the needy, by necessity they will reexamine their own motives behind gratitude and giving. And by observing conditions of squalor and suffering, they will conclude that they have a great deal to be thankful for and even a great deal more to share with others.

Prayer: For food and health and the security of our home, *we lift our voices in praise;* for the kitchen, the workshop, the sandbox which keep our minds active and our hands busy, *we celebrate your goodness.* Amen.

The Latest Word

The Bible

But as for you, continue in the truths that you
were taught and firmly believe. For you know who
your teachers were, and you know that ever since
you were a child you have known the Holy Scriptures, which are able to give you the wisdom that
leads to salvation through faith in Christ Jesus.
                                        II Tim. 3:14-15

In A.D. 303 the emperor of Rome, Diocletian, is-
sued an edict stating that all Christian scriptures
were to be burned. Obviously, the power of their
influence was a threat to the religion of Rome,
emperor worship. To stop the fast-growing church,
he reasoned, why not destroy its source of inspiration, the Bible. Twelve hundred years later during
the first quarter of the sixteenth century, Tyndale's
English translations of the New Testament were
burned according to a decree from the bishops of
the church. Only at that time, the printing press

was going full steam and was capable of reproducing a hundred copies daily. There was no way to destroy this new breed of Bible. Even today it is incredible how much opposition there is, particularly among ultraconservative Christians, to our newer versions such as *The Living Bible* and the American Bible Society's *Good News for Modern Man.* Are these newer Bible translations a threat to status-quo Christians in that God may become too relevant in human affairs?

Today, however, we live in tolerant times. Anyone in America who can read can have easy access to the Bible with no fear of persecution. This isn't our problem. Ironically, now that we have all this freedom and tolerance, most Christians are quite apathetic toward a disciplined study of the Bible. Why has it lost its appeal? Consider the following arguments: (1) The Bible was written exclusively for the past. God's Spirit was more alive to the prophets and the disciples. It fails to speak to contemporary issues like abortion and cryonics. (2) There are contradictions and errors in the text. (3) The Bible contains grotesque and outlandish stories and narratives, and is out of step with modern psychology. There are many contemporary books and novels like *Love Story* and *The Godfather* which are much more exciting and realistic.

True, many of these objections appear legitimate at first glance. But after a more detailed analysis, we will discover that (1) the Bible is a very human book. It exposes real issues and problems (David's adultery and Solomon's political corruption) which are universal and timeless. Although we cannot trace down specific problems created by technology in its pages, its truth as a whole speaks of love, responsibility, freedom, and faith. (2) The Bible's 5 percent errors and contradictions (created by human miscalculations), when matched against 95 percent error-free and consistent content, melt before the authority and truth of God's Word. Mark Twain once observed: "It is not those parts of the Bible that I don't understand that bother me; it is the parts that I do understand." (3) The Bible is broad in application. It treats the grotesque along with the beautiful. In fact, the psychological insights of the Bible have addressed emotional illnesses centuries before Christ! The books of Psalms and Proverbs are filled with legitimate guidelines for child development and adult maturity. Contemporary books and novels, as valuable as they are, only deal with a small segment of human nature (often without redeeming, hope qualities) while the Bible takes it all on.

The Bible can play an effective role in the happiness and security of the family. By choosing those selections which have immediate appeal and which stimulate open discussions, the Bible will live again —and so will we!

Prayer: Thousands of new books are published each year, Father. But what about a book which offers guidelines to all life's problems? Doesn't your Word fill the bill here? Give us the wisdom to see this. Amen.

Shifting into High Gear for Christmas

Advent

As the prophet Isaiah had written in his book:
"Someone is shouting in the desert:
'Get the Lord's road ready for him,
Make a straight path for him to travel! . . .
And all mankind will see God's salvation!' "

Luke 3:4, 6

In a sense the Wise Men participated in the first Advent as they star-trekked toward Bethlehem. Their anticipations were set on edge with the hope of Isaiah's prophecy: "Get the Lord's road ready for him, Make a straight path for him to travel." And for us, too, Advent spells preparation, the tuning up of our hearts and minds for the reappearance of the Spirit of the Christ Child for yet another year. Of course, our churches challenge us to pray longer, read our Bibles more carefully, and smile as if we believed that the angelic chorus were singing a top-ten record. This token form of preparation, however, falls far short and usually fizzles in meaning before December 20.

I think that if Advent is to mean anything at all to our home life, we must latch onto those qualities of the Christmas Spirit which will keep us going (spiritually, that is) at least until Lent. If our Christmas balloon is punctured by the after Christmas letdown, then Advent has been a failure. Too often we approach Advent from the angle of what we should do, not from what God would do with us if we were game. From a Nazi prison cell Dietrich Bonhoeffer observed: "Life in a prison cell reminds me a great deal of Advent—one waits and hopes and potters about, but in the end what we do is of little consequence, for the door is shut, and it can only be opened from the outside."

One possible highway we may travel during the Advent period is the way of hope. Let us call this approach hope with a cutting edge. As such, Advent becomes an unfinished construction project cutting a highway of hope through a secular jungle of despair and alienation. "Hope" is a frustrating word. It's like looking through a telescope at the planet Venus. We can see enough to know that something's there. But what, we can't be certain? This was Paul's mild frustration when he wrote: "For who hopes for something that he sees? But if we hope for what we do not see, we wait for it with patience" (Rom. 8:24-25).

Patience? Hasn't this become a lost word in our age? Possibly, a lack of patience alone has virtually canceled out any understanding of a spiritual hope in the life of contemporary man and woman. Frankly, many of us are afraid of the word "hope" because it is often associated with the experience of death. And death bugs us because it interrupts our exciting life, one throbbing with tomorrows on end —or so we think. Certainly, God wants us to enjoy this life to its fullest. Yet there is more to life than just secular living. Jesus meets us with this punch line: "I am the resurrection and the life. Whoever believes in me will live, even though he dies" (John 11:25).

According to Jesus, then, hope is what living is all about, and it is ours for the asking—or should we say for the trusting? That is to say, hope has an *eternal dimension:* trusting in Jesus' promise of an existence of moral stability and inner happiness within the context of his Kingdom. Hope has a *present dimension:* trusting in the power of Jesus' love to heal racial divisions and social injustices. Hope has a *future dimension:* trusting that the presence of Christ will linger with us to and beyond the end of this age of uncertainty.

So the cradle towers over the atom, the lunar orbit, and the computer, after all. For only in that cradle of salvation, made flesh to us in a distant past, lies the hope for our troubled world. And that is hope on the move!

Prayer: Isn't there more to Advent than *ad*ding up our good works and *vent*ilating our spiritual errors? Instead, doesn't it focus upon your Son's entrance into our affairs? O come to us, Immanuel. Amen.

Warning! Bethlehem Straight Ahead

Christmas

For God has revealed his grace for the salvation of all men. That grace instructs us to give up ungodly living and worldly passions, and to live self-controlled, upright, and godly lives in this world.

Titus 2:11-12

My dear God-rest-ye-merry-gentlemen(women) Christians, who imitate angels on stereo records and reproduce stars out of styrofoam and plastic:

So Christmas is acomin' and the geese are getting fat, and you've got your sights set on tinsel-town, Bethlehem, that glistens with heavenly moonlight and miles and miles and miles of hope? We can't blame you. We recall centuries ago when we made our angelic debut before the Bethlehem audience. How exciting it was for the celestial brother(sister) hood. Of course, as you recall, it was a celebration to end all celebrations, the introduction of the Christ

Child to mortals like yourself. Stars flashed with pride, the heavens exploded with hallelujah-style choruses, and you never saw a more shaken up group of shepherds in all your life.

But don't misunderstand us. We wish to make one thing perfectly clear. We're not here to reinforce your fantasies with an idealistic, gentle-little-Jesus-meek-and-mild piety. Although it has its place with children, with adult mortals, it's a harp of a different chord. Actually, the purpose of writing this celestial parchment is to warn you against the hazards that lie in Bethlehem.

Perhaps the most serious danger is the temptation (thanks to our adversary, Satan & Associates) to *embalm the Christ Child with irrelevance.* Although few of us up here (or is it out there?) possess PhD's in celestial psychiatry, on occasion our Heavenly Father has permitted us to wire-tap your unconscious thoughts. At this point many of you have been thinking, "Don't grow up, little Christ Child. We like you the way you are, so beautiful and gentle. For in growing up the Christmas star will fade, the Magi will pass into life, and the angelic chorus will cease to publish glad tidings about silent nights and first noels. Besides, by growing up you will be exposed to a cruel world. You will suffer and die. And that means that I, your servant, will have to suffer, too. You see, Jesus, I live in the twentieth century, and I want to keep my religion comfortable with as little responsibility as possible." Could this attitude in part account for the fact that toy manufacturers make the Nativity scene more professionally attractive each year?

Another danger we would caution you against during the Bethelehm celebration is the enticement to *bury the humaness of the Child*. By no means are we suggesting that, in your understanding of his mission to planet earth, you slice his personhood into sacred-secular segments. He was divine; but even more incredible, he was fully human, too.

Again, we will give you an instant replay picture of an unconscious motivation which many of you possess: "Religion is OK as long as we keep Jesus in his place. There he can keep tabs on our sins and keep occupied with the administration of heavenly affairs. But yank him into the dirt-grime-blood-sweat-and-tears of our place here on earth, well, that's too threatening to our man(woman)hood.

But mortals, that's why he came in the first place, to bring the authentic "us" out of the woodwork of our callous relationships and masks. He came to be more than one of the boys. Through a mastery of the hard knocks of life (temptation, suffering, and death) with his love, He became a real man. And through this love you can become fully human, too. That's the real message of Christmas!

Sincerely yours,
Angel Gabriel

Prayer: Christmas is here, Lord, and as usual, we're not quite with it. Sure, we've made all the secular preparations. But what about the spiritual ones? If it isn't too late, help us to make up for lost time. Amen.

Let the Sunshine In

Epiphany

The Word had life in himself, and this life brought light to men. The light shines in the darkness, and the darkness has never put it out.

John 1:4-5

After the Christmas letdown, each of us finds it extremely difficult to stir up enough enthusiasm for anything, with unpaid bills and income tax forms staring us in the face. Even our religion has a tendency to take on the blahs and our faith becomes like Job's turkey, so poor that it had only one feather on its tail and so weak that it had to lean up against a fence to gobble. Then someone reminds us that it's Epiphany time and we reply, "Sure, if you say so."

Epiphany? You know, it's that festival of lights where, as we drive away from the Nativity event, the rearview mirror blinds us with the light of the Christmas star; and we are reminded, "It's not over yet." Thus, Epiphany is a time for careful reflection on Christmas. Many of us ponder: "What happened? Christmas went by too fast, and here I am standing with that star-dazed look in my eyes." Perhaps this was the frustration of the Wise Men who, after the excitement at Bethlehem, wondered if that was all there was to it, a God-sponsored pageant with little hardcore meaning. Was that just another big-flash event written in the stars, just another played-out star plummeting to a splashdown recovery?

I think not, at least for us today. One could easily see how the Wise Men from the East, Gaspar, Melchior, and Balthasar, might make such a conclusion. For they lived in the Age of Pisces and according to astrology, it was characterized by death and eternity, which began with the rise of the Roman Empire. But we live in the twilight of the Age of Aquarius, which is supposed to be the pinnacle of civilization, the age of brotherhood and spirit and a thousand years of peace. Although biblical revelation may not jibe with astrology, there appears to be a close resemblance in this case. At least, we must agree on one score, the age which Aquarius promises is one of hope and of love. And that is definitely what the New Testament gospel has in mind. The only difference is that, although astrology's predictions are future-oriented and deterministic (it's going to happen, regardless), the Christian gospel suggests: "Why wait? Let it happen *now* through faith."

Such is the theme of Epiphany. With the key of faith, unlock the doors and windows of your hearts and let the sunshine of God's love in. This was the love that the Child in Bethlehem cast upon the fate of mankind and released him with a freedom that would never quit—the freedom to have a say in his own destiny and to love his brother as no brother had ever been loved before.

Again, we are blinded with the light of John's words: "The light shines in the darkness, and the darkness has never put it out." Arthur Gossip once observed: "Everything seems against it, yet it refuses to be killed." By secular means, we may attempt to dim the radiancy of its turned-on power, but somehow we inevitably fail. Essentially, God's love has always had the upper hand against prejudice and injustice. With this assurance, Paul affirmed, "There is nothing in all creation that will ever be able to separate us from the love of God which is ours through Christ Jesus our Lord" (Rom. 8:39).

Prayer: Father, may we keep alive the glow of the Christmas star and pass on its love to everyone. Amen.

MAKING LOVE
A FAMILY AFFAIR

JAMES WEEKLEY

Getting "the American family" together for a period of uninterrupted meditation may seem like Don Quixote's impossible dream. That's why these contemporary family devotions are so important.

Each brief, biblically oriented text pertains to topics of specific relevance to family members. Here are ideas for nearly an entire calendar year designed especially for family talk-times.

Improvement in family life starts with individual family members. These discussion starters encourage individual spiritual growth through reflective sharing periods. They rise above family hassles and invite introspection.

Strengthen your household from within through the "meditative power" of family readings. Shift the daily schedule into low gear at least once a week and be patient enough to listen to one another and to God's word.